Sweet Wolverine

A collection

of

brutal

truth

~~SWEET~~ ~~WOLVERINE~~

selected from worldwide submissions
by baraka noel
C Anne Gardner
Sean Taylor

with an introduction by Sean Taylor

SEVEN7H TANGENT

Published by SEVEN7H TANGENT in San Francisco, CA

Edited by Baraka Noel, Sean Taylor & C Anne Gardner

Book design by Sean Taylor & Baraka Noel

Cover Art by Jordan Saiz

Cover art and design copyright 2015

Contents

Introduction

Something is buried here:

We take a leap when we pick up a lit mag, or an anthology. A relationship begins with this stranger, this book, *Sweet Wolverine*. Perhaps one of the author's names looks familiar, or one of the title pieces causes you to shiver.

What are you looking for other than to shiver?

You're suspended right now, no doubt, here with me, leapt and hoping that these pieces, these authors, will catch you living.

There is something to the sound of breaking glass that catches you living, it perks up your shoulders, spurs the hair on *your most forgotten skin patch*. Some months ago, in some morning hours, baraka and I found the sound of breaking glass, hoping to catch life. He asked me what to do. I told him the bars would be closing soon. He said we should put together a lit mag. I said, yeah, sure, that's just talk, *everybody just talks*. He said *fuck you*, we're doing this.

I remember it being a wildly loud and chaotic scene, and I wanted to look a million places at once. At one forty-five Sunday morning, I wanted to make a book just like that moment. I wanted something excessively drenched in life. Instead, I told him, that we must make it good.

Now we have these forty-seven brilliant pieces and I'm thinking about *those shovel eyes in the front of your head*.

Start digging, there is something buried here. Help me get it out.

This is what great literature does. It exhumes. You're running down these lines, you're pushing details and characters aside, you're asking so many questions. *You're getting to the bottom of this.* I can tell you these authors are really letting you have it. *Trust me*, they have these wonderful scars as proof, *there's something below them too.*

This is how great literature feeds. *It goes both ways. You didn't call it treasure until we put the effort into burying it. And now here you are, going down and getting it.*

This is how great literature works. It's an exercise, it can't be that easy, we can't just come out and say it. *If you want to hear that you can go out back and break some glass.*

I wanted the best work I could find, baraka asked for brutal truth, *visceral honesty,* he said. We would go to readings and wring out what was left. We would get real quiet sometimes, and then say *I feel strongly about this.* It was a good feeling.

This is what we have to show for it, a book with forty-one authors, their work selected blind from all over the world. Their ages range from sixteen to early seventies. A sturdy book, bound with bodies *dying* to stay alive, and the barking sound that makes. They're something ferocious and buried mad, *so get digging.*

-Sean Taylor

Truth Is

I ain't wrote a thing I love in years.
Ain't loved a written thing since Breaking Bad,
but you can't tell me I don't owe somebody something.
Biggie died at 24. 'Pac at 25, which means
I've squeezed more juice out of this here skin suit
than some folks change the game with. Who can say
where justice is? All I know is next week
I have to turn in four separate papers
or the last two years of my life become a joke
I can't explain the punchline to. So let me move
these fingers some. Let me get a little right before
I settle into this oblivion. You ain't heard? This rock
stay spinning, son. The Mayans got it wrong so now
I gotta build a future with my tongue and fingers. Thanks. And
hey
guess what? There's only two flavors in this whole ice cream
shop:
you either case a ruddy river or outbluff an apocalypse
of soccer moms, and either way you gotta get for real
about a dental plan. I know this life gets even harder.
I know the state of my crumbling teeth don't turn a blue
sky gray for anyone but me, and some shit does. You don't
believe me? Ask the folks on my street what they think
about a camera on a cop and watch the storm clouds gather.
Listen man: I'm not sayin I'm not grateful for the way the
world
refuse to let me go, the way it calls on gravity to hold me
to its chest despite my lack of fucks, my unkind eyes and
how I foolishly insist on my own sovereignty. But I'm just
sayin:
what kind of fallen thing is Justice when the world don't stop
for Mayan prophecy, don't stop for my broken heart,

or empty plate, my cowardice; the way I'd rather masturbate
than venture eye-contact? What kind of fallen thing is Justice
when I get to walk around knowing that the world won't even
stop for any wasted, poemless sunrise I spend drunk and
handcuffed
laughing at police, but 2Pac died at 25, Biggie 24,
Trayvon Martin, 17?
You can't tell me I don't owe something.

-Robert Zenz

The Abyss

For Omotayo, who drowned herself in the Hudson River

PART ONE: GUILT OR THE AUTHOR
INVENTS A STORY TO COMFORT HERSELF

mother was a giant
huffing moon

planting a kiss under soil
and when an orange tree

grew, she plucked the body
and let light fall through

dimpled skin   later
the silver fin appeared

a hammered thimble cutting
the threat of water

the girl threw out the old gossip
of her body like an anchor

slipped off tired skin
and swam and swam

until dusk was a purple scarf
hiding the hole in her neck

until morning came
and she was gone

~

PART TWO: EMPATHY OR THE AUTHOR
ATTEMPTS TO RELATE TO THE VICTIM

the truth is blunt as a noseless shotgun
I have brushed my fingers against the lips

of that quiet world, fantasized the smack
of a city bus against ragdoll limbs

bug-eye beneath the cool rush
where sound is muffled with cotton

but I am an adult now and I can count
the reasons to lift the morning covers

can call on logic to push the boulder from
the body's mossy center, for example, taste

buds, it is date night: lamb biryani, mustard fish
on payday, scrambled eggs when money is low

another way to look at hunger: softening towards
what might be named compassion, what feels

like a secret: everything is holographic, strained
through the mind's distorted sieve to be made real

I didn't know this when I was seventeen, and still
sometimes, I forget how to be kind and kind enough

to myself to know that tomorrow a note may arrive
fly right up to the window in a bird's beak, a sign

but you came like an arrow through our
morning, we were going to escape the city

down by the river where life is windy
and green and sneaky and summer-sweet

you walked right up to the abyss
let it fill wherever water could creep

bent limp mastering childhood's dead man float
tell me it's the mind's deception, this cruel way

of coming to know   a woman
the water tried to reject
            the water wants no hold
 it pushes us up towards
                    our rightful place
         the sky   inside
the burdened body
         the bones
                 of once belonging
         floating alone
         in the mouth
                 of dirty river
         where nothing
is worth saving

but I saw you,
         Omotayo
         and exited my shell
I saw you,
         Omotayo
and we were in

a classroom

I was handing
you a book
saying wisdom
can come

through any body
any vessel

even when it is ugly
most things,
          when you brush them off
are ugly
          swing the axe down the center
                    sinful, even
I can tell you what I've done
what I can't unsee, what I know
          to be wrong
          and still,
                    I am thirsty
          still,
                    I can name my hunger
                    in the belly of another bear
          or beast   or angel that appears as a shadow
          on the living room wall
          I have failed so many times
          it would be wrong to look you in the eye
still, I want to touch

          everything
          everything
 is holy: *you*   -Caits Meissner

Prayer of an Atheist

I feel stoic. Kind of empty. Lonely and bitter and no matter what I do to distract myself I feel like I am withering on the vine. I'm desperately, and constantly, seeking something different to make myself feel. Different books, different movies, projects, music and alcohol. I feel trapped and suffocated and burned by a world I'm strangely not participating in. There is something that has gone horribly awry and I have no clue what that is. The walls are closing in and no matter how much I fight and flail my arms I feel almost sold out, incomplete and dangerously wrong. I keep hearing the same songs on the radio, the same commercials for insurance and the same ticking clock telling me that my life just reduced by one more agonizing second.

I read something terrible today. It was an article online that said that early man, 12,000 years ago or so, had to work about twenty hours a week to sustain survival. Twenty hours of hunting, fishing, scavenging and finding shelter. The rest of the time was spent in idle contemplation, looking at the stars and taking in the beauty of a shiny new planet. The article did not really discuss what early man did in his free time. I just made that up. The thing is, what else would there have been for a limited thinking being to do with his time? I cannot even imagine looking at the night sky in a world without electricity. I will never see it in my lifetime. I will never walk dirt that is not owned by someone.

I read this article and then looked around me. I then looked at my watch and realized that my half hour lunch break was over. I turned around and saw the angry face of my co-worker who wanted to use the computer I was on. I logged off and stepped back into the warehouse, slapped on my back brace and slid my leather gloves back onto my oddly dainty hands with their perfectly trimmed fingernails. I wondered what early man's fingernails looked like. I looked up at the halogen lighting in the massive room and pretended I was looking at the sun. My week was almost half over, and I realized that I had worked well over twenty hours this week already. If I was early man, this would be the weekend.

Twenty damn hours. I walked to the stack of pallets that needed to be loaded onto the truck and thought about the fact that I had not seen the sun today except on my drive in to work, and I realized that the sun would be down before I left today. Then a very aggravating thought came across my mind. I looked at the walls, the plain concrete floor, the raw steel beams supporting the impossibly high roof of the warehouse and thought, This is progress? How was this progress? I wake up early, I shower and drink horrible coffee. I eat overly processed cereal while watching the Fox 5 morning news team smile and pretend that the world they are reporting on is not complete shit. I get in my truck and I drive twenty miles in bumper to bumper traffic and I go inside a building for eight and a half hours. When I come out I am tired, and I get back in my truck and go home where I watch sitcoms full of the same boring people I have to suffer all day at work. I heat up soup that came from a metal can made months ago in a factory in Mexico. I then watch the Fox 5 nightly news team. I do this all for a paycheck that lets me live long enough and just well enough to know that I need it.

Need it. Do I need it? I need food. I need shelter. I need water and vitamins. I need clothing. I need transportation. I need windows and indoor plumbing. I need granite countertops and an espresso machine. I need a plasma screen television and ninety channels full of people telling me what else I need to buy in order to be happy. I need instant messaging so I no longer have to talk to my family. I need a computer to watch pornography so I don't have to go outside and find a mate. I need a $6000 watch to know how much time I have left to live.

Where does it stop? In ten years I will need a robot to wipe my ass, or some other handheld device to do something that my phone will eventually do two years later anyhow. Right now I am working twice as hard as early man, and yet I am enjoying half of the planet that he enjoyed. The only benefit that I can perceivably notice to living now instead of 12,000 years ago is that I live longer. So. What. It doesn't mean a god damn thing if my longer life is miserable, mediocre and scarily irrelevant.

I realized that I had been looking at the pallet in the middle of the warehouse for entirely too long and snapped back to reality. I looked at it more closely. It was wrapped in stretchy, shiny clear plastic. It encased a stack of boxes that contained black, shiny boxes that did stuff. Some played music. Some made that music play louder. Some routed the signal of the music to the things that made the music louder. None of it was actually music. I think it was that realization that really put me over the edge. None of it needed to exist.

So what now? What do I do with this new realization? *What now?*

I looked at the metal wire encased clock on the boring wall in front of me, you know, the kind you see in gyms so that they don't get busted by a basketball or angry fork lift operator. The kind you can barely read because it is so protected. I looked at the clock and realized that I had just spent four minutes thinking about how shitty life really is. Four minutes gone, never to be seen again. Four minutes I could have been making love, eating spicy foods or hiking through a forest.

With four minutes I can make a paper airplane. I can draw a picture, make art. Four minutes is enough time to look at a meadow and truly, not superficially, but truly appreciate it. In four minutes I could have been king of this world if only for a second. But now, staring at the clock on the wall, encased in wire so it doesn't break, I realize that my death is now four minutes closer than it ever has been.

Am I just a clock? Am I just encasing myself in protective wire so I don't die? What good is a clock if you can't see the numbers because of some stupid, fucking wire? What good is a life if it isn't being lived?

A desperate panic overtook me then, and I realized that at that moment I could have killed someone. I realized that I had wasted thirty-one years of good life on crappy public education and a dead end, unfulfilling life.

And when I got home from work that evening, I looked at my surroundings, my carpeted life, and just for a moment pictured it as a cave, a dark dripping natural rock formation with nothing but a fire to keep me warm and entertained. Would I be happier? Would I feel relevant again? Something tells me no, because the human condition is one that will always want to find better ways of making itself irrelevant. The industrial revolution made manual labor irrelevant. The computerized age of automated cars and bots will soon make the human oversight of those machines irrelevant. And someday very far down the line computerized bots will make thinking irrelevant. Then what? Humans can shrivel up and be blown away with the wind, their purpose fulfilled? A virus only evolves when it encounters an organism it can't yet infect. Is that the fate of humanity? Are we just stuck evolving until the next great calamity presents itself to us?

I can see now why so many people in this life turn to religion. They sit and feel good about their miserable life wasted watching Maury Povich because they are told that something greater is waiting for them when they die. They justify living life stuck in traffic, not seeing the sun and eating month old freeze dried dinners. But that justification can only take the human race so far. Someday all the lying that we are doing to ourselves is going to bite us in the proverbial ass.

The construct of an advanced brain who realizes his own mortality required the belief of something beyond itself. Well, I want to choose that something, not have it chosen for me. I choose food, travel and a woman whom I can fall in love with. I choose to abandon the things I have built around me as safety and embark into a world I have only seen through the flickering lights of a television screen. I choose those things because they are the most wonderful human things I can think of. They are the same things that early man craved. Do you think he craved an eight cylinder crew cab truck? I'm betting he did not. I'm betting he would pass on that truck for a good view of the sunset over a mountain valley.

This is the reason I am leaving. If I don't do this now I fear I never will. Goodbye job, truck and apartment, and hello pre-columbian architecture, deserted fishing coves and flagrant acts of rapscallion art. Like my ancestors twelve thousand years ago I will embark with little to my name over the arc of the horizon, to lands yet unknown.

Consider this my two weeks notice.

-Jay Nelson

Stage Dives From the Throne

" & we make a lot of noise, because we love each other"
       – A Silver Mt. Zion

Kids like us aren't designed for distant observation,
so you won't see anything from the back of the room
tucked safely away from all the dangerous things –
from far away, the only thing anyone can see is a frenzy.

Come closer. Step into this,
waltz with the maelstrom,
come   closer.

The photographers will show it dangerous,
still-life portraits of high speed collisions
where the knuckle & the tooth become as one,

& landlords charge us twice the rent for each revival,
or the flashing lights of patrol cars come to leave us blind,
but we congregate. We huddled-mass, we breathe free,

with feedback squall & peals of thunder
our awkward lungs scream out a hallelujah,

call down electricity from on high. All these twitching
limbs & torsos come together all at once –

here, an angry young man with a locomotive in his chest,
here, a girl in denim & rust with hair dancing like serpents,
here, a boy with a railroad track for teeth,
        a boy more bones than muscle & blood,

our society of square pegs & lockpicks,
a roaring fire, a full-moon howl,

building our cathedrals out of half-stacks
bought on bad credit, strings de-tuning endlessly
from the tension, & volume, always fucking volume;
how there is never enough because the LOUD is drowning out
our teeth chattering dismay from the outside

& if we can hear anything at all we can still be
haunted by our thoughts, & in this house of worship
there is no room for the dry coughs which would cast us out.

& faraway photographers will show it dangerous,
like the floors are sticky with blood,
like all we are is war, but come closer –
step into this.

See how our hands are always open,
        even when they ball into fists.
See how our mouths fly open
        & pour out light on everything.
See how our bodies climb & climb.
See how we build our temples to the sky.

                                        -William James

Sleeping Giant

As you lay dying, a full arena chanted and screamed your name.

You hailed from an era of 300 pound Dead men in black walking the top ropes of wrestling rings like acrobats. Sledge hammer wielding Machiavellians, clashed with brawling alcoholic rednecks, while jam packed coliseums brayed for blood.

14 years old, I watched Air Benoit take flight, a barrel chested ballerina soaring head first into rib cage or not. Sometimes it was the sickening thud of cranium smacking canvas.

It was a double murder suicide. Friday you asphyxiated your wife Nancy. Saturday you did the same thing to your 7 year-old son Daniel. You left a Bible beside both bodies. Sunday you hung yourself from your weight bench, familiar Bible nearby.

Your brain resembled that of an 85 year old Alzheimer's patient. You had advanced dementia. Were the first known case of CTE. A brain disease caused by years of untreated concussions.

When you called Chavo, said Nancy and Daniel had food poisoning, did you choke on the words? Did you almost ask for help? "I've done a bad thing Chavo. There are goblins in my brain Chavo." Did your pride prevent you from doing so?

That same pride which caused you to pump steroids into your veins so you could compete with
stronger, younger men?

Your bodies were found the next afternoon. That night your wrestling family broke character, told tearful stories about your life. They described you as "quiet and
gentle." A "peaceful man." Said Daniel was a mini version of you. That you didn't just love him, you adored him. Then the news reports.

Vince McMahon described what happened to your family as a tragedy. Was he referring to lost life, or lost dollars? Was it out of nobility he ordered your merchandise removed from shelves, your matches deleted from public domain, all commentary mentioning you edited from existence. Was it out of nobility he made
Chris Benoit the forbidden name of professional wrestling? Owen Hart free fell 30 metres and the show went on, his lifeless body wheeled past other wrestlers.

Difference is when a wrestler dies they are a tree in the forest. Nancy and Daniel Benoit a car bomb in Central Park. Vince implemented safety rules, drug testing, all to extinguish their sound.

Chris we never saw you as human. Chris you were a crash test dummy laid low during impact testing. Chris you were an Underdog Superhero chiseled to perfection in a pharmacy test tube. Each squeal of adulation driving the needle deeper.

-Daniel Patterson

Shower Thoughts

the only thing worse than growing old and jaded
is the sobering realization
that you already are
when the whiskey can't numb your soul and
when you can cum with a straight face and
when you can measure time by cigarettes smoked
it stops being poetic

-Khari Waits

Champagne

The sinkhole in Lee's backyard started small, as a divot of sand that could've been written off as some anomaly of erosion or the handiwork of a disgruntled gopher, if only it hadn't expanded with such hunger, minute-by-minute, day by day, until it encroached upon the dwarf dogwoods and the wrought-wire credenza at the edge of the patio. The pit's walls fell hyperbolically, a study in mathematical derivatives like the bell of a trumpet, sinking faster and faster with each inch inward toward the center, which itself fell into darkness—no bottom, no light. No nothing.

Lee stood above the hole, his head reeling from the champagne he'd drunk for breakfast. He probed the precipice with the toe of his sneaker and imagined the stomach-turn he'd feel upon tumbling headlong. If he did, this would all be over, all of it. Instead, he sank backward into a wire patio chair.

On the far side of the sinkhole, rust nodes were forming on the lawnmower, blades of grass grown up around it, half-hiding the wheels. Lee didn't have the energy to bring the mower into the garage. This morning, he'd hardly had the energy to pop the cork on a bottle of champagne—which he had been drinking daily for breakfast—much less the energy to sweep up the scattered fragments of the dozen or so formerly-identical bottles of champagne he'd thrown against his garage wall. Rings of white sugar efflorescence remained on the concrete where the champagne had evaporated.

The progression of the sinkhole went like this: day 3, salad plate; day 4, dinner plate; day 5, pizza pan; day 6, failure of cookware analogies; day 9, kiddie pool; day 11, swimming pool; day 14, all-consuming void.

Lee poured out the dregs of his morning's second bottle of champagne. A force like wind or gravity seemed to draw the liquid away from the walls of the chasm and straight down the center of the hole in a perfect golden stream. The darkness in the bottom of the hole had a strange substance to it. It was not regular darkness, which is the absence of light, but a sort of inverse light, a black shroud, a darkness of substance. Lee opened a third bottle and poured it out, and again the same weird gravity drew the liquid in. He followed it with a fourth, because fuck it, there were five and a half more cases of the stuff in the garage. Every single bottle had an identical custom label with his name on it, plus Jaime's. A couple days ago, he'd sat for an hour trying to peel off the labels, but the adhesive was persistent.

Lee was passed out by noon, hung-over by one, drinking off his hangover by three. He'd fallen asleep in the lawn chair again, and his peeling nose had worsened. He awoke to find the wrought-wire credenza teetering precipitously at the threshold of the drop. He nudged it with his toe. Watched it fall. Lee drained the sun-hot dregs from a bottle lying sideways in the lawn, then tossed the bottle down the sinkhole.

Inside, he stared at the blinking red numbers on the answering machine, and pressed delete, delete, delete. In the garage, he tugged on Jaime's old gardening gloves (a size too large for his own hands), and brought out a wheelbarrow and a shovel.

Lee dug up the flowerbed—the coneflowers, the tulips, those yellow daisy-looking things. When he had the barrow full, he wheeled it to the edge of the sinkhole—now the size of a modest pile of minivans—and tipped in his load of flowers and earth. The dirt disappeared. The hole did not lessen; nothing seemed to have filled in.

Lee worked until the dehydration gave him a headache, and then a bit longer. He decimated the raised-bed veggie plot. He uprooted the roses, tore out the petunias, deracinated the chrysanthemums. When the perennials and edibles had all been destroyed he tossed the shovel, wheeled the barrow to its death, plucked off the gloves one finger at a time and threw them overboard, dusting his hands together as they fell. In great overhead heaves, he chucked the wire patio furnishings piece by piece.

He made trip after trip: comforters, afghans, trash cans, desk lamps, wireless phone handsets, instruction manuals for wireless phone handsets, needlessly-saved boxes and shrink-wrap for wireless phone handsets, coriander, cumin, cayenne, black, pink and white pepper, The Rise and Fall of the Third Reich, War and Remembrance, tubes of burnt umber, ultramarine and gamboge, an ottoman, a queen-sized mattress, queen-sized box spring, queen-sized wooden bedframe. By dusk, the flagstone slabs of the patio itself were being swallowed.

Lee climbed on the coffee table and hung from the ceiling fan until the fixture ripped free from the drywall. After the fan, he wheeled out the fridge. The photo albums that used to sit on the coffee table had long since been tossed, as had the anise-flavored toothpaste that only Jaime brushed with and the decaf beans that only Jaime brewed. Lee even tossed the crates of champagne, though he immediately regretted it, and then un-regretted it when he thought of how it was the last thing with Jaime's name on it, but in the end regretted it even more when he awoke the next morning with his tongue as swollen as a broken toe and a murderer of a headache, and there was no booze to be found except a half-bottle of anisette, also formerly Jaime's, which Lee had missed in his drunken cleansing of the kitchen cabinets.

He drank the anisette standing at the kitchen sink, watching the sinkhole expand. The back bedroom and the sunroom both listed at the edge of the hole, their foundations already half gone, sagging an inch lower with each passing minute of the ground falling out from below. Lee busted out the kitchen window with the butt of the anisette bottle, and tossed the bottle through the window hole.

He searched the knife drawers but could find no remaining knives, as they'd already followed the butcher's block and the silverware. There was no rope in the garage, no belt in his closet. The prescriptions had all been emptied from the medicine cabinet. The stove was electric, and Jaime had taken the car when he'd left.

Lee lay on the empty living room carpet, his body framed by a sun-faded rectangle where the sofa had sat for years. After a while, a car pulled into the driveway and killed its engine. The doorbell rang. Lee didn't move.

"Lee?" Jaime's voice. The sound of the key working the lock, the swath of light from the opened door cutting across Lee's eyes, brightening the blood red of his closed lids.

"Close the door. I have a headache."

"You're hung-over?"

"Close the door."

"I won't bother you. I just came for a few things."

"There aren't any things."

"Don't worry, none of your things. None of our things, even. Just a few of my things."

"There aren't any things."

"What do you mean there aren't any things?"

"There aren't any things at all." Lee pointed to the backyard. He rose and followed Jaime, wrapped his arms around Jaime, held Jaime tight from behind as they stood together before the sliding glass doors.

"It's good to see you," Lee said.

"You're drunk."

"It's so good to see you."

Jaime slipped the knot of Lee's arms as easily as Houdini might shrug off handcuffs.

"I'm just going to go get my things."

"I told you—"

But he was already disappearing down the hallway. Only there was no hallway to disappear down. The floorboards had splintered and the carpet hung like a loose tongue into the gaping maw of the pit.

"What've you done with my stuff?"

"I told you."

"What've you done with the bedroom? Where did the sunroom go?"

"I told you."

The kitchen wall collapsed in a roar of snapping timbers. A section of the roof followed, and a breeze entered from the back lawn, which was no longer a lawn but just a big expanse of nothing.

"You're pathetic."

"Don't go."

"I'm going."

Jaime's car pulled away and the sound faded into the distance. In an explosion of tile and burst pipes, the bathroom crumbled and fell. The roof beams splintered and slipped and did not crush Lee to death, but went down into the black. Somehow, everything had fallen around him. Lee was trapped atop a spire, a tabletop-sized hunk of living room suspended above the black. He lay back on the carpet, waiting to feel the floor go out from under him.

-Christopher Mohar

YOU'RE NOT SPECIAL

everyone has a dead dog just like everyone has a brother
just like everyone has a wound in their side from that accident
with hot water from earlier this afternoon & everyone's been in
hot water or used it to cook noodles or drowned in it, you're
not special, everyone was born in new york in a hospital named
after the mountain where a god handed down his hebrew words
& in the hospital everyone was born screaming & premature
with an epidural in their mother's spine, everyone lies,
everyone
lines up to die, everyone cries ink in private, you're not special,
everyone's skin blisters when burned & if not, everyone's dead
dog's ashes were kept in a tin in their parent's basement for
years just like everyone & their brother went to scatter those
ashes in the park where you used to walk her as an excuse to
smoke pot & leave your cold house behind & she'd turn back
her giant dog head & judge you as you coughed & shook into
your burning
palm & all that's left of her is the ashes you & your brother
scatter from a tin & the hebrew you butcher canting memories
of her youth before she grew too sad to walk & you were young
too once & now you are old & have taken providence over the
dead as you sit with your brother on a park bench in silence or
you sit alone tending the wound in your side or you sit & scald
these old letters into your box of light.

-Sam Sax

GREAT NORTHERN HOUSES

In this town the houses move. All of them. That's not cause they're trailers on wheels or cause the ground shifts. The houses just move. Slither along in the dirt, slide a few feet here and there, but always end up back in their original spots. Shift in their lots like they're fat men in recliners, trying to get comfortable.

But as God is my witness, I never knew houses could jump.

Sometime last September I was grappling a two-year-old tree in my backyard, tearing at a tough bastard branch too low on the trunk, when my friend come running up my side yard. Eyes wide, brow drowned in sweat, face slap red, he stopped, hunched over. Back heaved each breath. "Jerry!" I said. "The hell you been doing?"

He held his hand up, palm out.

I let go of the branch.

Still hunched over, he planted his hand on his thigh and looked up. "Running."

"From your house?" Back then he lived five miles from me. He nodded. "You got a car, yeah?"

"Crushed."

"Wha'd you junk a four-year-old car for?"

"I didn't crush it." He stood straight up. Arms hung at his sides. "House did."

"Sure it did." Every yard in town's at least an acre big. "You park your car too close to it?" Every house in town's surrounded by no less than ten feet of dirt.

A safety zone.

"I parked it at the foot of the driveway, Tradd." He drooped his eyebrows. "Like always. Way more than ten feet from the house. Then I come back from camping in the woods, out behind—"

"Yeah I know, by your house. Where else you camp?"

"Well so I come back. Car's crushed, house is gone."

I bent down. "Gone." Grabbed the branch.

"Must've jumped." I yanked the branch.

"Like hell it jumped." Fought again.

"Whatever it did, it's—

"The branch tore from the trunk. "It?"

"It's gone. My house is gone."

I weighed the limb in my hands—"I dunno, Jerry"— then dragged it off. "Maybe you're drunk"—I threw the branch in the woods aback my yard—" or maybe this is like the time your son was"—some brush grabbed my foot—" 'attacked' by your other son's lab." Worked my foot free.

"You think I'd run five miles on a hot soup day just to pull your leg?"

"Well," I turned around, "you didn't have a problem hiking in three-foot snow to get me rushing over to examine dog bites." Walked back toward him.

He stuffed his pockets with his hands.

"Can't forget when you gave me that fake winning lottery ticket either."

"I've got photos, Tradd."

"Almost got a damn heart attack."

He held up his phone.

"I don't want to see your pictures."

"Course not." He dropped his phone back in his pocket.

"Let's say your house is gone, though."

"It is."

"File a police report."

He squinted, mouthed the words.

"Missing persons, I guess." Patted my shirt to my forehead. "What you want me to do?"

"Get in your car"—he pointed to my front yard—"and help me look for it." Wiped his brow.

I laughed. "What am I, a dick?"

He pulled a cigarette out his pocket and lit it.

"Not wasting my gas, I can tell you that."

Jerry sucked that paper stick like it was a soda straw. When he blew out I would've swore on sight the temperature was five below.

"You just gonna stand there—"

"Mmhmm."

"—and stare me down?"

He shrugged."How many those you got left?"

He slid the pack out his pocket. "Ten?" Flipped the top, nodded. "Five minutes each."

Shaking my head, I walked up my porch—"Course you got it timed"—and opened the sliding door. "You go on and blacktop your insides," I said. "I'm gonna shower." I stepped inside, locked the door behind me, walked on down to my master bath a front.

Some people say when there's thunder it's angels bowling. Next sound I heard must've been God crashing down the bottom of a hundred-story elevator shaft. Then the ground heaved—shook me down to the deepest hollow spot between my ribs—jellied my guts—rattled my teeth—everything jumping—zigging and zagging a front me. I fell over—knocked my head on a doorknob—pulled myself up by that doorknob—pressed against the front window.

Jerry's thin house, right there.

All windows broken, doors off their hinges, siding loose and swinging about, weathervane gone, back deck a shambles. Wood and glass and brick and concrete everywhere. "Jerry!" I said. His house crunched down upon itself and stretched up and—I shit you not, it leapt right off the ground, higher than the shaft that bested the Almighty. It arched long and far past the edge of the neighborhood.

I stumbled to the back of my house. Pictures and books and plates off their shelves and all over the floor. Sliding door was cracked. I flung it open. "Jerry—your house, out front!" A faint thud rung out. Glass dropped from the door. "Was."

"I knew it wasn't an earthquake," he threw his cigarette down. "Let's go!"

"Doubt we can catch it."

"It took an hour or two to get here. It's moving slow."

"Could've been hopscotching all over town."

"Could also be jumping around randomly." His cigarette smoldered. He stomped it.

I wondered where his wife and sons would sleep. Loved them like family—but not at my house, their sons always shouting into their gaming headsets at people they never met. And his wife, she'd kill him. Then she'd cling to me and my wife, maybe even try to redecorate our place, till we killed ourselves.

Jerry popped his jaw.

"Fine. Go round front."

At my car I stopped by the driver's door, dug for my keys. My head turned to paper, moved by the wind. I swayed, but managed to stick the key in and grudge my door open. I leaned across the seats, unlocked the passenger door. "Plan of attack?"

Jerry sat down shotgun. "You saw where it went." Buckled in.

I stared at him. Then the steering wheel. Shut my eyes. "Over the far end of Meadowbrook." Jerry's house. "Northwest side." Jerry's thin house, right there.

"Past the trees?" Big forest of pines there.

I nodded. Cranked the ignition.

He whistled. "Maybe six miles?"

I nodded. Backed out the driveway. My car groaned over the crater his house had created. I shifted into second. Drove for Meadowbrook's entrance. "We find your house, what're we gonna do?"

"Lure it back."

Empty, treeless dirt everywhere. "This i'n't a dog, Jerry. A strip of bacon won't work." After six years, only a quarter the lots had been built up. "Hell. Doesn't even work on some dogs."

Jerry stared down his window.

For the first time I lusted for the town outside my subdivision. But Meadowbrook's roads fought to keep me in, forever winding and straightening and curving and intersecting —snakes fleeing from men trying to stomp them. My head papered out again. I swerved, clocked a mailbox.

"Tradd!"

I blinked slow. Exhaled, smirked, cocked my head. "Smashed my skull on a fucking doorknob when your shitbox house landed afront, Jerry."

"It's not a shitbox," he muttered.

Jerry waited till we finally passed Meadowbrook's always-empty guardhouse to tell me what to do. "Turn right," he said at the light for Highway 190. "Northwest's aright."

"I know it's aright."

"Then stop looking aleft."

"How long we'll be on 190?"

"I don't know." He tapped his armrest. "What's behind the trees behind Meadowbrook there?"

"Off northwest?"

"Yeah."

"Pelican Park, I think. Or it's close."

He tapped his lip. "Could've landed near the soccer fields."

I turned right. "My daughter's playing there today."

Highway 190's pale tar road top burned bright into my eyes.

"Think the house hurt anyone?" Car shuddered. Pothole.

"Your family?" I said.

"All at the in-laws'."

"Soccer field, then."

"Mm."

"Probly not. They'd see it in the sky there."

Pelican Boulevard snaked its way from 190 back to the parking lot afront Pelican Park's soccer fields. At the closest field people stood along the edges. Game was suspended. Looked to be all were. People stood everywhere. Jerry and I stepped out the car. Gravel underfoot.

My wife spotted me—"Come for Jerry's house?"—and walked toward us.

My daughter talked with her teammates nearby.

I nodded.

"Landed maybe fifteen minutes ago," my wife said. "Jumped a couple minutes after that."

"Everyone ok?"

She nodded.

"Where'd it go?"

"Toward My-Why, looked like." Mile-Wide Lake, which everyone called My-Why, sat off K Ten Street—about seven miles from Pelican Park—where for the most part it drowned no one and did a poor job sheltering lovers on its wide grassy banks that tumbled acre over acre.

I kissed my wife on her cheek. "Thanks, babe. Be back soon."

Jerry and I clambered into my car. I snaked back to 190. Turned left, tore down the cracked-out highway. Streaks of brown and black and grey blurred together; white and yellow stripes mixed in. Pine trees forever on both sides. And maybe fifty yards behind them, carless, houseless neighborhood streets. Paved. Cracked. Waiting. Not knowing they were abandoned.

"Is it worth chasing down?"

"It's your house." Very few cars out.

"Will it even be fixable?"

"Fixable? I thought you said it wasn't a shitbox."

"I'm sure it is now. We somehow get it back to my lot, I hope I can sell it."

"You moving?"

"Maybe." Jerry scratched the cinnamon stubble on his chin. "Friend in Chicago's working on lining up a job for me there."

"Man. Uprooting your family."

"Three hours east ain't uprooting my family." He pressed a limp fist to his temple. "Nothing here in Allena."

"Can't go camping round Chicago."

"Can't go camping round here either."

"So where's the job?"

"They're pulling down the woods behind my house."

"Where's the job?"

"Big corporate accounting firm."

"You account for that private school here."

"They don't account enough for me. Everything's stuck here. Or draining."

"Draining?"

"God. More pines."

"It's pines everywhere, Jerry. You told me always has been."

"Remember the local news folk and politicians all talking about that—well—not an actual pump—but all them talking about how jobs were gonna get pumped into town?"

Stoneybrook on the right. Roads paved years ago. They knew the other ones were abandoned but they thought they were good. "That was '02, right?" Tricked by half-built wood skeletons.

"Those shitty ads they ran?" Snakes fleeing from men trying to stomp them.

"Poor-chosen image. Sure a pump can pump in. But it can pump back out, too."

Or was it the men were getting dragged by the snakes? "You gonna take that job?"

"It's not set yet. But yeah. Be able to buy a new house for my family? Yeah I'll take it."

More pines forever. "One that's not a shitbox?"

That was the first time I ever saw Jerry flip me off.

"All looks the same anyway," I muttered.

"What?"

"Chicago's gonna catch up, or down, or whatever direction it is. Eventually."

He ignited his lighter, released its fork.

"What'll you do then?"

"I don't know. But I'll ride the crest now." He cracked his thumb. "While there is one."

Two miles down K Ten we come up on Jerry's house sitting by the distant closer lakeshore: a small block way off, plain as that ball in Pong. I drove to about fifty yards from it. Stopped. We stepped out onto the grass, stalked up. Lions casing an antelope.

"How we proceed?" Jerry breathed.

"How should I know?" I whispered. "I never hunted."

"You're Cajun, yeah?"

"Wasn't raised it—and Granpaw was a tired, smoked-out, mellow old man when I come along."

"You bring bacon?"

"The hell for?"

"Rope?"

"Rope?"

"Yeah."

"Would've been twine on the house, Jerry."

"Eh?"

"Wouldn' been worth a damn!"

Now I never heard people say If this house had ears—but I swear Jerry's house heard me. Soon as I shouted, it crunched down upon itself, stretched, leapt straight up—almost —scratched the sky. It crashed down in the middle of the lake, pushed water lurching far up onto the shore. A splashing thud rung out as the water slunk back down.

"Fuck."

That was the first time I ever heard Jerry curse of his own. Even then he muttered it.

"That about tears it?" I said.

"No shit."

-Matt Matrisciano

89.

Back to the oceanic lands with dinosaurs and muted pears
In your hand. Turn up the volume on color and violence;
Awash in a sea of information. How hard it seems to be
To give in to your higher being, the one asking you for
Peace and blindness lest the answers fall-out and get
Stumbled-upon.

Oh, what a glorious day this is; fish in the sea, birds
Riding the wind – the calm that comes before any
Storm is enticing but fleeting. We have few seeds to
Give – few rocks to bleed. Take me out, to Ohio or
Nebraska, to a calmer land than this one. Here I see
Them, gulls, swallows, kestrels, minnows, salmon,
Barrels of it, oh my.

-Benjamin Biesek

Precious Child

Special snowflakes grow up to be nothing
but special cogs in a special machine
Cry alligator tears and buy faux fur,
organic monoculture bananas,
organic shampoo, organic clothing
Green like cash, paint every label green
You can paint coal clean. Nuclear power
lets us dance all night like Carmen Miranda
Now it's American dreams we're fracking
Problems don't exist if they stay unseen
We've bought everything green. We're proud owners
of the wasteland sinking like Atlantis
Who will eat honey from the last beehive
Who gets rich when the last elephant dies

-EK Keith

29

It is the summer before I turn thirty. I am riding shotgun on the Oklahoma turnpike, passing a one hitter with the sun roof open. The trunk holds tall boy PBRs and a fat bag of Blueberry Kush. My father always warned me, old man D.A.R.E. style, that rock bottom would sneak up on me. That my life would fall apart when I least expected it.

The Nissan is going 92 mph, the driver a girl that can channel Hunter S. in Las Vegas like a ghost. She swerves off for roadside attraction diversions, signs with large red letters: "fresh fudge". There are four of us in the car. We are all houseflies to Missouri tourist shit. It takes twenty minutes for us to maze through the hillbilly schtick, to get back in the car and keep driving.

We get to the Tulsa library, an hour late for a big zine fest. I help set up, then sensory overload wander off on foot into Tulsa. I eat Popeyes chicken, saying a prayer to the poor bird that died for my sins. Wander on to a Conoco, buy a Red Bull, then down until I find a man with a roadside missionary t-shirt shop. He has one design, a black shirt with a globe with continents made of black and white faces, with the words "Kill Racism, Not Me". He says he feels like he is called by his God to sell these shirts, so I agree to buy one. I give him ten dollars that I don't have to spend. I am half a mile away from the library. The Nissan pulls up, the girl hollers for me to get in. We get back to the library. Crack PBRs and drink them in the parking lot. Head back inside to sling more zines.

It is the summer before I turn thirty. I once told a man I heart loved infinity that this summer was the summer I would get pregnant. That I wanted kids, and wouldn't wait past the summer I turned thirty. A man whos sweet lips never tasted of weed, a tongue that got giggly on a few sips of rum. I told him I was done with worlds that swirled when I closed my eyes, that I wanted the responsibility of a weighted womb. The summer before I turned thirty, it was my line.

It is the summer before I turn thirty. I am curled naked against a man whose body I do not know. I am drunk and high and the metal in his nipples surprises me.

Tipsy, then wobbly, on light beer, then vodka. High, sitting on the couch, making out with this man. Talking about the Universe. I know him as well as you can know someone on the third date. Each date has lasted hours. The Universe is an expansive subject. He asks if he can stay, already drunk enough he shouldn't leave. The request is just formality. He just beat my ass at Dominion, a super nerdy card game. He isn't leaving.

I am in bed with him. Drunk but not shitty drunk. We are naked. He tells me to "get my hand on that cock". I reach down, find more metal. Realize I have no idea how piercings work with condoms. I ask. He says it is fine. He is drunker than I am. I worry it is more likely to break. I realize it is fine. Planned Parenthood is only four hours away. I am not going to have a child the year I turn thirty.

The condom doesn't break. My phone is growing a text garden from him, a man who always walks in with PBR and blows his green smoke into my mouth. A man who promises me that this is going to be a good summer.

It is the summer before I turn thirty. It is complicated, this summer. This place.

The man who blows smoke in my mouth is not the only man in my world. The paperwork for monogamy is rejected wadded up muddy in the floorboard. I do not have interest in buying that model. I will not sign their lines. Tucked away in Facebook is a novel of mutual explorations, makeshift monologues exchanged with a man who I have only bone marrow respect for. A man who I never smoke or drink with, whos body is a temple and who expects me to treat mine the same when I am with him. A man who I have 54,000 words worth of conversation with. More than my thesis, the one I finished the year I made the proclamation about this summer, years off at the time, the summer before I turn thirty.

I have road trips and pine tree sticky smoke and beer on my tongue and the smell of sex on my sheets. I write daily, I spend my days touching words. My home has "Bachelorette Art Palace" written in Sharpie on the mailbox. It is the summer before I turn thirty.

Three years ago, I quit school, came back home to have babies, to build a foundation from seafloor fossils and call it new. I came back home to find comfort in the known. This summer, I have two crazy perfect jobs, no ring, a phone full of texts that make me smile, and lips that tingle from blunt tips. My last fat zine had the dedication: "To the men who have slept with me and never tried to make me their wife."

Years ago, when my fingers were so quick to draw lines in sand, I would have thought this was apart, that this was busted seams. I would have been on my knees, scooping up the pieces. I still have moments of panic. This is not what I had planned. This is not the summer before I turn thirty. My father's warnings have me whispering "danger", but this sure tastes as close to happy as existential angst can be flavored.

I guess this is the summer before I turn thirty.

-Amber Culbertson-Faegre

The Unique One Climbs The Mountain

I'm at this acupuncturist
because I haven't slept
because I was watching
porn because I am
stressed because I was
porn because/stressedbecause...

                    "Symptoms?"
It asks me as though everything I thought
I just said I just thought...
Thirsty?
I drip back like the first drop of coffee
at the smug mug of someone
who just "wakes up like this"
bobbleheading empathy-
zombie with extra teeth--
"I'M THIR-STEE?"
I repeat slower to its lab coat's bottom button.
"But--in the beautiful sense of the word: for tea...romance...
meaningful work--What chakra is that??"
The acupuncturist has seen worse.
"Did you help them?"
It employed cupping remedy. Would I like to lie down?
"Yea..But...were they still thirsty?
Because I want to be more functional
but no less lost..." I start repeating: "But--" but it cuts me off
squeezing this jar on my kneecap--"Is something in there??"
I ask, imagining I am a bug trapped in my own knee,
the acupuncturist has to diagnose me as
flying or creeping to prescribe

smashing or letting go of
the lives I wanted, who
I was going to be
and with
before I grew
up and gave into--
Do I have sciatica? "Yea."
Really I'm just so tired, I can't tell it....
I haven't slept since I last had a bedtime,
can't remember the last time I went to sleep
instead of passed out and I refuse to
trap the pupa in my face now,
will not shutter my pupils
before they chrysalis
the humor out
of all this
shit
I DON'T NEED
YOUR CHI AND HERBS, DON'T NEED
A DOCTOR OR EASTERN DOCTOR--I AM ADDICTED TO
MY HAND!
SPONSOR ME-- In my mind the exam table is a psychiatric
gurney; I writhe and scream, snap the straps...
FUCK YOUR NEEDLES YOU NEED TO PULL
A HATCHET FROM THAT PINCUSHION
CASTRATE MY GRIP--STOPSMILING!
STOPIT! I AM NOT YOUR PATIENT
I AM THE UNIQUE ONE!
A CHARACTER
LIKE THAT KID IN THAT MOVIE CALLED A NUMBER...
(FORGET WHICH ONE JUST NOT 1) I SEE
SEXY PEOPLE EVERYWHERE WHEN I NEED PEOPLE,
IMPERFECT BOUYS NOT FAKE BLISS,

REAL RELATIONSHIPS LOST IN A SEA OF BODIES
END OF BINGE WHEN I JUST MISS MY EX--
AND NOT JUST SEX--HOT TODDIES...
OLD FASHIONED DRINKS
WE DIDN'T TRY BUT
MIGHT HAVE
IF I--"All done."
                    Fwoop!
 "OW!"
It has removed my kneejar, unpricked
my jerkoff thumb throbbing like a just a came cock.
I let my eyelids drop for the first time since puberty
woke me to the fact I wouldn't know inner-peace
if it spanked my ass and called me bad...baby...
I climb down the bed thing and look out
from the peak of Mount Bay Area
Alternative Medicine yawning
my battle cry: "OOOHAHHHmmm..."
a semi-erotic intone I am sure topples
like an avalanche upon the assent
of adjacent rooms' patients
         less parched than
the Unique One

.

                                        -Abe Becker

Delilah's Broken Jawbone and Scissors:

If passion is
 the fruit of madness
We have already stained our mouths
purple with desire
Destiny is the suffering
        we relish, together
I don't want
their silver pieces; I want my sanity back.
I want to forget the bow of your lip
and the soft hair
on your arms.

In this moment, before
you drift into sleep
We embrace
Hating and loving
each other
in equal measure
Punch drunk   with affection.
Our bodies turn to ash
like a field
ravaged by 300 burning foxes.

-Leigh Cuen

Some Things That Happened After Laura Went Back to Ohio

It was 7:18 p.m. in San Francisco on a Sunday evening and Tommy was drunk. It was his third day of existing in a world that no longer included Laura, and he was ill-equipped for it. The best he could think to do was hit the downtown bars with abandon, in search of some special new doom to distract him from his present circumstances.

He eventually ended up at the Brown Jug, finding it as dreary and slow as everywhere else. Bartender Frank looked haggard and tired. He wordlessly served Tommy a beer, then went back to cradling his head in his hands, his elbows propped upon the bar. There were a couple of old guys to the left of Tommy's stool and a woman to the right. The woman looked far gone, drinking something clear from a pint glass that sat on the bar in front of her. She was middle-aged and gaunt, but not completely devoid of charm. Tommy sat next to her and halfheartedly attempted to engage her in some nonsensical conversation, but had no idea what he was saying and she wouldn't have cared if he did. They sat there in their own separate miseries, sipping their drinks in silence. Even the jukebox was dead.

At some point Bartender Frank lost consciousness. He was crumpled upon the bar like a broken puppet, snoring and moaning like something haunted. Nobody was immediately in need of a drink, so they let him be. A group of young Filipino men stood outside smoking, sneering, and drinking beer from tall cans in paper bags. They glanced in now and then at Frank, whispering to each other with mocking voices. One of them, tall, lanky and cruel eyed, walked in and stood leering over the bartender's inert form, making obscene gestures as his friends took pictures with their phones. The man poked Bartender Frank's temple with his finger, calling him a sad ass motherfucker as he did so, until one of the old guys at the end of the bar got up and waved his cane. The Filipino man grabbed a six pack of something from behind the bar, made a grand obscene gesture meant for everyone in the room, then ran off into the night with his friends, their laughter fading into the darkness. A few minutes later, Bartender Frank stirred, coughed, shook himself off a bit, and started wiping down the bar as if all were right with the world.

It was around then that Tommy felt drunk and weary enough to go home and dissolve into sleep. He stepped out into the dark and walked up Hyde Street, making his way through the gauntlet of night people that crowded the sidewalks. Dreck peddlers on every corner, hawking useless, broken things, women selling whatever was left of themselves, some with nothing much to offer, but demanding compensation nonetheless. Tommy stopped at a corner, waiting for the light. A group of Mexicans stood smoking and drinking from paper bags. A pickup truck was parked at the curb, a woman in the driver's seat chatting with those assembled. She raised her tallboy in Tommy's direction, cigarette dangling from her lips. Tommy gave her a tired smile and a nod. The light changed and he continued on.

A couple corners later Tommy was stopped again. To his left the woman from a few blocks back was idling in her truck. He gave her a weary little wave. "Where you going, baby?" the woman asked.

"Home," Tommy said.

"Why home?"

"Bed," he replied.

"Lemme give you a ride."

"It's just a few blocks."

"Lemme give you a ride anyway."

"Why?"

"I'm lonely," the woman said. Tommy considered a moment. That was one of the few things in life people tended not to lie about. He stood there weaving on the sidewalk for a moment and then climbed into the passenger seat.

The woman looked over at him and smiled. She was maybe forty years old, weathered, but attractive enough in such a way. She held out her hand and Tommy took it in his own. "I'm Heidi," she said.

"Tommy," Tommy said.

"I'm drunk," Heidi said.

"Me too."

"Where am I taking you?"

"I don't know."

"I mean, where do you live?"

"Oh. Just on Bush. Halfway between Polk and Larkin."

Two minutes later Heidi's truck was in front of the building. "Thanks," Tommy said, reaching for the passenger door's handle.

"Look," Heidi said, "I got nothing to do. I could use some company."

Tommy paused.

"I got a place we can go," she said, "no big deal."

Most of Tommy knew it would be best to follow through with his plan of sleep, but the relentless little part of him that felt the need to ruin any possibility of a peaceful end to the night was powerful. "How far?" he asked.

"Only a couple minutes across the freeway."

"Freeway?"

"Yeah, I got a room in Daly City. Dude gives me a deal at his hotel."

"Daly City's a little ways out there."

"I'll get you back in one piece, baby. There's a guy I gotta meet around here in a few hours anyway, so I gotta come back." Heidi placed her hand on Tommy's leg, caressing it through his jeans, her hand eventually coming to rest on his inner thigh. "I'll make it worth your while."

"Well, you know, I don't have a lot of, you know, money right now," Tommy said.

"How much is not a lot?"

Tommy made a fuzzy attempt to take stock of his current financial situation. "Like sixty bucks, maybe."

"We'll make it work, honey." And then they were on the 101 headed South. Heidi handed Tommy her beer as she caressed his thigh. Tommy took a drink and returned it to its place between her legs.

Heidi's phone played a Jay-Z song and she answered it. Tommy heard a man's voice, harsh and impatient, but couldn't make out any words. "Yeah, baby, I know, I know. I'm with someone right now," Heidi said to the phone. "We're gonna hang out a bit and then I'll head back over there. Gimmie like an hour, okay?" She ended the call. "See?" she said to Tommy, caressing his leg, "I gotta be back in your hood in just a little bit."

Tommy nodded, unconvinced, and gazed out the passenger window at the lights flashing through the darkness; cars, buildings, parking lots. Heidi turned the radio to a country station, and George Jones sang about living and dying by the choices he'd made. The whole world suddenly felt like a sad country song, a kind of purgatory. Tommy felt lonely, in spite of Heidi's hand on his leg and the musky smell of her filling the space around him. The great sadness of everything seemed too big and impossible to comprehend or overcome. He thought of Laura, and wondered what she was doing and who she was doing it with.

"What's your story, babe?" Heidi asked.

"My story?"

"You look kinda forlorn and all."

Tommy kept his face to the window.

"Where's your girl?"

Tommy made a noise like a broken laugh. "Ohio, I guess. But she's not my girl anymore."

Heidi lit a cigarette. Tommy hoped she would offer him one, but she didn't. "What happened?" she asked.

"I didn't want to move to Ohio."

"Ohio? What would you do in Ohio?"

"That's what I said."

Heidi laughed a little laugh and squeezed his thigh. "Yer alright, baby. Don't you worry about no bitches. They ain't worth it."

"Yeah," Tommy said, taking the beer from between her legs and finishing it off.

A few minutes later they pulled off the freeway and they were somewhere Tommy didn't recognize. Daly City or South San Francisco, he guessed. Everything felt particularly desolate. The world was reduced to parking lots and abandoned looking buildings. Rows of sad hotels and lonely gas stations. He didn't see any people anywhere.

"Almost there," Heidi said.

"Can we stop by a liquor store or something?" Tommy asked.

"I got booze in the room."

"I need an ATM, though."

"Well shit, you coulda told me that earlier."

"I forgot."

Heidi looked annoyed as she lit a cigarette. She made a few sharp lefts, pulled into a gas station, screeching to a stop near the entrance. "Hurry up then," she said.

"Can I get you anything?" Tommy asked as he stepped out of the car.

"A pack of smokes. And matches. And a few extra twenties for the room. For the deposit." Tommy nodded and entered the little store. A large bald man with a great black beard stood behind the counter, watching a tiny television. He greeted Tommy with an unfriendly stare and watched as he pulled a hundred dollars out of the ATM. Tommy was now forty bucks short for rent, but he figured he could transfer some money from one of his credit cards that wasn't maxed out. He grabbed a bottle of red wine with a screw off cap and bought it along with a pack of cigarettes. When he got back in the truck, Heidi was talking heatedly on her phone. "Yeah, I know, I know. Look, he's back." Heidi tossed her phone on the dashboard and snatched the pack of cigarettes from Tommy's hand. She ripped it open, lit one up and they hurtled out of the parking lot.

They drove another few blocks and turned into the parking lot of a particularly beaten down hotel. The lot was dark, only a few cars were scattered about. Light shone through the thin curtains of a few rooms. The hotel sign was broken, so Tommy couldn't figure out the name of the place. Only a neon "E" blinked into existence at random intervals. They came to a stop in a dark corner of the lot. Heidi reached into her bag and pulled out a joint. She lit the thing, took a long drag and offered it it to Tommy. "Here, baby," she said, "have some of this." Tommy took it and had a few big drags. He felt immediately lighter, a kind of empty peace welled up within him. "You like that, baby?" Heidi asked. Tommy nodded in the dark. "Have another hit." He obeyed and was filled with a welcome numbness.

"What is that?" he asked.

"The good stuff," Heidi laughed and took another drag, then returned what remained to her bag. "Look," she said, "my room's right there!" Tommy looked to where her finger pointed, some undetermined spot on the second floor of the building.

"Okay," he said.

Heidi got out of the truck and Tommy followed, though he would have preferred to just sit in the warm darkness, smoking whatever it was she had in her bag. "Alright, I need the money now," Heidi said. "Sixty for me and another forty for the room." Tommy pulled out his wallet and rummaged for the bills. "And a credit card."

"Credit card?"

"For the deposit. No big deal, you get it back when we leave. They don't charge nothing to it." Tommy gave Heidi the wad of bills and his ATM card. She counted the money and pushed it deep into the pocket of her shorts. "Alright," she said, I'll pay for the room and we'll be all set." She pulled a ragged five dollar bill from her bag and handed it to Tommy. "Hey," she said, "there's a 7-11 down on the corner over there. Could you go get me a Diet Coke?"

"Diet Coke?"

"Yeah, the Cherry kind if they got it. Meet me back here at the truck."

"Okay," Tommy said, gazing uncertainly about the vast parking lot, seeing only dark. "Which way?"

"There," Heidi pointed, "on the corner."

Tommy tried to walk in that general direction. He got through the parking lot, reached the sidewalk and didn't know which way to go. All directions looked equally pointless. He chose one that he felt was slightly less hopeless and lucked out.

When he reached the end of the block there was a shabby little 7-11. He went in, bought a Diet Cherry Coke and headed back.

When Tommy returned, the hotel somehow felt even more desolate than before. He wandered about the parking lot and couldn't find Heidi's truck. He criss-crossed it a few times over to no avail. He managed to find the office, but it was as abandoned as everything else. A sign in the window said "Closed. Back at 6 a.m." Tommy turned and scanned the empty parking lot once more, standing there with the Diet Cherry Coke in his hand, suddenly understanding that Heidi's truck wasn't there and wasn't going to be.

Tommy stood there, stupid, helpless and alone. He walked to the sidewalk and sat down. He pulled out his wallet. He had three dollars. He'd left the wine he bought in the seat of the truck. He was at least ten miles from home in a neighborhood he didn't know. He felt sorry for himself and cried a bit. He pulled his phone from his pocket and the battery was all but dead. He punched in Laura's number. She didn't answer, but he knew she was up. She was always up. She had night terrors and never slept until the sun rose. He listened to the recording on her voice mail. It was the first time he'd heard it, as it was the first time he'd called her that she didn't pick up. Listening to her voice telling him she wasn't available right then was lonelier than anything he imagined could exist in the world. "Hey," he said after the beep, "it's me. I'd just really like to talk to you, is all. If you'd give me a call when you get this, I'd appreciate it. It doesn't matter what time it is." Tommy ended the call, knowing it wouldn't be returned. He figured he'd try and get a cab, despite the fact of his three dollars. He imagined they could work something out. The battery on his phone gave out as he searched for a number. He walked back to the 7-11, went inside and asked the man behind the counter if there was a phone he could use to call a cab.

The man shook his head.

"You have to have some kind of phone," Tommy said. "I just need a cab."

"Employees only," the man said.

"Okay, well, can you call me a cab, then?" The man looked at Tommy as if he were orchestrating some kind of scam.

"No. You have to buy something or leave."

"Look, man, I'm kind of stranded here."

"Leave or I call police."

"You can't call a cab but you can call police?"

"Yes."

"That's fucked up," Tommy said, turning away.

"*You* fucked up!" the man shouted after him, as if he were casting a curse. "*You* fucked up!"

Tommy walked back to the sidewalk. He stood there listening to the absolute silence of things. He looked in all directions, and none seemed any better than the rest. He looked out across the sea of dark and stepped into it.

-William Taylor Jr.

Love Poem/~~Love Poem~~/Why I'm afraid of or don't deserve you

i am too dirty to belong
to anyone but myself.

and isn't that inherently filthy:
the need to be possessed
by someone?

a boy is using his pelvis
to push my voice into a place
not even i recognize.

all i can think of
is how you wouldn't.
how we never even kissed
till i made the first move.

on days i am a manic swan
black as the bodies that raised me
the moon makes every glass screen
in my room a river

of blood. i flirt with memorials
while praying for bird baths.
still, you speak to me of song

of this voice you believe
everyone needs to hear.
silly me. not every

white boy looks

at me the way you do
will tell me to spread
what you call feathers.

not every white boy
listens for the same falsetto.
some believe there is beauty

in the way i curdle or screech.
and isn't this all disturbing:
how you tell me i am
deserving of the sky

how you end conversations
with be safe, how the sky
becomes your name,
how i fall from it
and land somewhere
you will never be?

a phone app can tell me
i am 5 min. away from being
buried alive while keeping
my love silent. vibrating
beside a body unfamiliar to itself.

and isn't that fucked up:
how a text message
becomes a graveyard
next to a graveyard?

this morning every article
of clothing, every brackish

jewel sliding down my face
every sound i owned
is a feather he plucks
with enjoyment.

i leave his apartment counting
the few blessings i can:
at least his voice didn't

call me a nigger.
at least what i swallowed
was sweet. at least he wasn't
you. he could never be you.

-Joshua Merchant

HOARDING

Your house stuffed with junk you've never
Coped with, the reservoir of that failed
Marriage, though he's long dead, this is all
You have to show for it, an aviary of
Finches, a lost daughter, the geodes
Of memory, how you descended into the
Canyon on foot on the hottest day.

Your car is full of overflow, the trunk
Bulging like the garage, the storage units,
The house next door you bought to cram.
The providence to store the future.

Here's a pocketbook of caution,
Articles on decluttering, tracts on how the
Heart is burdened, how nothing useless
Shall be enticed. You turn to a catalog of wishes.
What more, what more can you gather.

-Joan Colby

INVISIBLE SAFETY NETS

I'll forgive you when you admit you were never going to pick up my call; when you admit you were intentionally sticking your head only half way inside the oven; when you admit that you lied to a man who had broken your heart again that you weren't really 5150, you were just really fucking high.

Not that you HADN'T just swallowed a handful of Xanax and Klonopin chased with a couple of shots of Bulleit, I mean hell, you've been riding that sled for years dear; Emeryville PD made sure that detail was correct because the next three weeks wouldn't have happened if they hadn't.

In turn I will admit:

That yes, it had occurred to me that you could take it. That yes, it had occurred to me that you told the heartbreaker you were offing yourself because you were sure it would break his heart because it would make him call you later to make sure you were okay, because it would make him kinda care in the way that no one else cared because they couldn't keep going down this road with you, never mind that he is the same kind of ambitious, cynical alcoholic you are, the same kind of jaded striver who is just one blow job away from the cultural lottery and because of that, you never imagined that he was actually a person of substance and caring underneath that, that he would really sound the alarm; that a suicide safety net actually had been laid out beneath your ledge, and that once activated, there will be no turning it off.

You know that they are going to put safety nets underneath the Golden Gate Bridge now. There will be no way to have that direct line of sight from the railing straight down to the water.

You know eventually, there is going to be that first person to try it anyway, thinking they can somehow jump far enough out over the net, or that the wind will catch them and they will fly to oblivion. But in fact, they will simply then become the first person to get caught in the net.

Can you imagine how that is going to feel?

Laying prone and essentially unable to move in the netting, no doubt bouncing up and down in the shrieking Golden Gate winds beneath, the hungry lapping currents below, waiting to be hauled up like the catch from a fishing trawler.

Yes, I imagine you would know how that first person is going to feel. I'll forgive you when you admit you jumped without looking for the net.

-Paul Corman Roberts

One Last Time

My sister's in the middle
of her second divorce
but this time there's four kids
and millions at stake.
They've been working at this
for a year and a half now
and it seems like they're
no closer to an agreement
on how to actually split up.
Maybe they know how the
lawyers egg them on with
all sorts of bullshit about
what you deserve and what
you're entitled to; maybe they
know and they just don't care.
Maybe they both know it's
their last time to fuck with
each other and they're gonna
take it real slow, make it last.

-Richard King Perkins II

Conductor

but waking next to you is like bathing in honey, only to realize
that instead of oxygen, the air is composed of infinite tongues.
i'm saying you do heavy things to me. & how you hum in the
morning. your buzz thickening until the whole of the room is
contained in the sound of your you. the sound of you breaking
the horizon is so loud it turns red & breaks people ears. in this
way, i'm saying you are like a sunrise that prevails over sound.
& when i see you standing next to fire i become jealous of the
way the heat touches you. lapping over you without effort or the
burden of self. i want to make a grand gesture, so i say, we are
here but somewhere a fire starts itself. i'm saying the fire
always wins. & when our house is on fire & the storm is
electric, i will dig a hole for you to lie in while i stand in the
rain, head tilted back, mouth & eyes agape. i'm saying i will
grow larger as the branches of electricity travel towards the
earth. with arms outstretched i'm saying i will not let you get
electrocuted.

                                                        -M.G. Martin

Where the Bees Are Going

Their yards were full with clover, their gardens with wild flowers. Everyone in the town hummed happily, from sunup to sundown. It was true, what they said about the townspeople: they sang with sweet, strong voices, but when they spoke, they wheezed. It was a slurred and syrupy sound.

One rainy day, everyone in town felt a need to sing. They turned their heads towards the sky, and when they opened their mouths, bees poured forth and became furry, yellow-black, shifting ropes of notes, respected by lightning, rising beyond the clouds. Some townsfolk climbed their ropes, never to be seen again.

The air was thick with pollen when the coroners arrived. They found silent bodies filled not with blood, but with honey. Ah ha! said one of the coroners, as though he had just solved an ancient riddle. They sneezed as they cut samples of honeycomb from chests and put them into little jars.

-Ori Fienberg

MIXED FORMULA

You have no faith in the words of others. Even your own thoughts are an endless stream of fraudulent ticker tape. Occasionally a person speaks and you listen. Usually it's a woman. A morsel from such a source can still sound digestible, but you might be making that up for spurious reasons, or for the hope of comfort you imagine might come from burying your hypothetical head into her hypothetical bosom, whoever she might be, with her half overheard sentences trailing off into the darker corners of a bar for the terminally sad. That was the last time your ears pricked up, wasn't it? Where did it happen? You've already forgotten. You've embraced the jaundiced view. You started out hopeful enough but never encountered depth that didn't make you want to drain the pool. What made you always yank the chain that held the plug? Why were you suspicious of content, and the verbal elaborations people used, to point to something called 'themselves'? You were an early opponent of too much information, we'll give you that. You were in the vanguard of withdrawal. Now you sit in a soiled bathrobe with the hood pulled up, like a defrocked monastic deposited in a downtown Oakland condo, the view sealed off with tragic curtains. You're a dour creature. And then it happens, the dormant machinery of your life cranks up. Light is present, and it's glaring. You can't access your bearings and you're glad, although 'glad' doesn't quite capture it. You're captured. She comes out of nowhere, the one place you forgot to look. She makes a sizable offer. The sheer scale of it makes it non-optional, or so you think. Actually, you've stopped thinking. A silenced mind, the goal of mystics, the trademark of happiness; it is yours in the split second that follows her saying:
"Undress me."

You don't know her. Because once you know a person, once their material is spilling into your life like four rooms of unpacked boxes, do they ever say 'undress me' in that tone of voice? And then quite unexpectedly you have a sense of déjà vu, and you realize maybe you do know her, kind of. Wasn't it your friend Alec who introduced you to her back in the day? Wasn't that the woman with the clammy handshake, the triumphant cleavage, the long legs? Weren't they married? They probably were. Alec probably introduced you, he probably said "this is my wife, Sylvia." He probably had a proud look. Alec had too many proud looks for his own good.

Perhaps they tired her out.

Right now, she's wide awake.

"What are you waiting for?" Sylvia says.

Do you even know where you are? Whose room is this? How did you get here? You think she drove? That's certainly possible; she's got the wheel, that's for sure. Did you tie up loose ends before coming? Isn't that what dragged you down in the first place, loose ends, the firing squad of ongoing tasks, attributes of real adult life? Which reminds me; where's your mother, did you forget about her, your only surviving parent...did she escape your notice? Convenient; putting your mother aside, while you do what exactly?

"Start with my blouse," Sylvia says.

It's a vintage blouse, light blue, prim, almost victorian. Her manner seems at odds with her appearance as if she's crossed from a drawing room in a Jane Austen novel into a nineteen-seventies soft core movie. Are you going to lift your trembling hands to those buttons? Why do the words hope chest keep springing to mind? Can you find a graceful path to Sylvia's breasts, and not lunge like a starving man for a scrap of food. This is a challenge you are up for I'm guessing, something to get you out of the house. Your mother managed the house, raised you kids, worked damn hard too. Someone had to pick up the slack, given your father's, shall we say lackluster work ethic. Did you leave your elderly mother at the bus stop, the wrong bus stop maybe? Was that deliberate, a design to facilitate your desires, now that they seem to be back? What if she's irretrievable, that mother of yours? What if she never gets home? Won't you ask yourself how you could have misplaced her so convincingly?

Sylvia's blouse is off. You may be responsible for that, unless she grew tired of waiting and did it herself.

"My bra, can you help with that?" she asks, which might be a clue. What does this clue reveal about your commitment, your initiative, your sense of responsibility, about what may have happened between you and Sylvia, about the possible location of your mother, if she is still with us, if she has not yet gone from this world? Was your mother once in a room like this, a dark room, a room off the beaten track, taking a break from being beaten down? Was there another man, one different from your lethargic pop with his petty tyrannies? In a musty room like this? Your mom, the competent hands of a stranger on her, the dexterous hands of a hard working man, who could manage, who could lead, lead your mother to a place like this, remove her garments, and her smiling, an expression of delight filling her usually melancholy face? A man who knows what he's doing at last. Might those have been your mother's thoughts? You are in strange terrain and bras can be a tricky operation, isn't that so? Hooks and what have you. You see Sylvia's breasts. They have made their way out into the open, free of confinement, a wild and blooming garden. You had filed her away under: wife of Alec, wet handshake. And now that same woman brings you to life. Did you help? Have you ever helped anyone? In the end, did you do your fair share?

Is that how Sylvia's breasts came out, as a result of your good effort?

Will there be a funeral for your mother if the worst comes to pass? Of course there will be a funeral, if they can find her, to bury her that is. She will have to be tracked down first. Even a dead person must be discovered and returned, in order to be laid to rest. You know that.

"You can touch me," Sylvia says.

-Peter Bullen

Childhood

It's like when you finally get to borrow the swimming goggles and you see a kid pooping in the public pool wotta let down total rip-off completely creepy full-on gross so you all quickly pack up and head for the car the blacktop so hot it's like magma and it's agreed that you'll stop at the Thrifty's and run in for a 10 cent scoop of ice cream you get bubblegum then yours melts and runs down your arms into your armpits and your beach towel is soaking wet it has dog pee all over it and you get all the gum in your hair and your little brother is crying again and you're being blamed for it and where is the goddamned dog now and now your nose is bleeding again from the heat and your allergies and you're crying too because none of this is fair and wait until we get home and the belt comes off and starts swinging and outside it's 110 and the car has no air conditioning and all the windows are open and everyone is either screaming or crying and even then you can remember thinking that someday you would be an older person done with the day-to-day struggles the chaos and strife of what was your daily life retired and smiling and calm maybe even a grandparent quiet and beloved

-SB Stokes

A Challenge to War

Your blood spikes make Tarantino
run. The warriors call it true
blood. Your blood sticks and licks a man's
skin as it takes away his dreams

and drains his consciousness. War, I'll
ask the questions of you that most
dare not. It was mad men who invited you here to poison the
world's cup. Did you ever see a
man torn apart by malicious
metal? How about a bullet's

foul caress? Have you been a witness to the distress of a man
made newly blind by an arti-
ficial shooting star? The watchmen
call it an omen of screeching

dissolution. Only on sil-
ver screens, you say? It's the same for
me, dear War. But I know enough.
We are lost when a man kills our
children in a school. But we dance
when our bombs take the souls of our
enemies' sons. You've taken eve-

rything from us: The cure for disease – physical and spiritual,
technology for peace, and lovers lost entanglements. With

you alive, there are no babies
for the women who love men who
drowned at sea. My fury is a

clot in my blood. Endless War, I
challenge you to a duel. I
pray we'll duel with words. Is there
ever anything about you
that is just? Or are you only
for devil's play?

-Eric Allen Yankee

Horn Man

"have dominion over the fish of the sea and over the birds of
the heavens and over every living thing that moves on the
earth."
 Genesis

at the cocktail party
the wealthy rancher
boasts of his acres,
his herd of longhorns,
his wife, his life.
high roller, businessman,
county commissioner,
he's a big deal, he brags.
one gold tooth glimmers
in his mouth,
a sly glint sparkles in his eye.

he tells us about a side business,
selling the horns from his steers
to barbecue restaurants, collectors
of cowboy memorabilia, and frankly,
other big shots like himself.
people can't get enough
of those horns, he swears,
then explains how he takes
the old steers, ties them
to a tree in the woods.

the coyotes come first,
make the kill.
the buzzards are next.
lastly, the ants
that pick the bones
and horns clean.
no muss, no fuss,
the rancher smiles,
rocks on his heels,
downs the last of his bourbon.

-Christopher Woods

Stomach Acid

Your ghost has been
dragging me down
for nine years.
My heart is concrete,
painted red trying
to pass the test.
And still, some nights
you rattle my ribcage
so loudly I can't sleep.
Let us both rest.
You must be
as weary as I am.

-Kristin Ryan

Jasmine Leung

Ever since our mother's marriage had fallen apart with her most recent husband, she had made it clear that my brother was the golden child, placed on a pedestal too high for me to ever mount. Maybe it was because I was the lovechild created between her and her ex, and there was just so much pent up frustration and resentment toward him that I was viewed as her only outlet.

So I guess it was a shock to her when she dragged her feet down the carpeted walkway to find my brother in the funeral casket instead of me. It didn't make any sense to her, which was understandable, since he had always been the one with the perfect looks and excelling grades, surrounded by friends and cheerful smiles. But she never saw what I saw since she was always working the shifts till dawn. She was never able to see the universes shredded apart, hidden underneath his long sleeves. She was never able to see the lit cigarettes, held between shaky fingers, pressed desperately between lips to alleviate some of the pressure felt by society around him. She was never able to see him hurriedly fan the smoke away as a key scraped the lock of the front door, or see him rush to reorganize the spilt medicine cabinet. He was squeezed by the looming future surrounding him, and it had finally become too much.

I cried, as did everyone else in that room, but I cried more because it was expected of me. It's not that I wasn't sad, because believe me, I definitely was. But I couldn't honestly cry and let all my emotions and restraints go in the presence of people who didn't know him like I did. Not in front of the people who didn't know how much he was suffering. Not in front of the people who sobbed and acted like they needed him when I needed him the most. Not in front of the people who always ask "how are you?" without really meaning it. Even his best friend never knew something like this was going to happen, only I knew, and maybe I could have done something to prevent it. This was the one regret I had.

I went to school the following day, and the day after that. When my friends asked how I spent my weekend, I told them I attended my brother's funeral. The way their eyes widened and jaws hung off the hinges told me they had not expected that response. They were expecting something lighter, something not as raw and as real as death.

I knew the question that was lingering on the tips of their tongues. Everyone wanted to ask, "How? How did he die?" But they all seemed to think better of it and instead gazed at me with a look of pity followed by whispers of, "I'm sorry for your loss."

I think they were half expecting me to tear at the seams in broken sobs, and half expecting me to venture into a monologue about how great my brother was, but I surprised them yet again with silence and a shrug.

It wasn't until the third day at school that I finally felt the impact of his death. I was seated at the back of the classroom, taking a test, when the panic attack pounded into me, as if I was standing underneath a violent waterfall.

I was there, yet I wasn't there. I was feeling, yet my eyes were void of any emotion. In a room filled with a dozen people, it was quiet, yet the silence was deafening. All I saw were the backs of heads, but it felt as if all eyes were fixated on me, scrutinizing every inch of my being with hard, calculating stares. Suddenly, I felt like I was unable to breathe. I forced my chest to rise and fall, but it was as if my lungs were stuffed with cotton. Tension and anxiety bubbled up and swelled within me, and my chest began to burn with the desperate need for air. I had to get out of here. But before I could rise from my chair, the thunderous vibrations of laughter bounced off the walls and attacked my ears like a raging cacophony. I reached into my opened chest and plucked out the cotton before stuffing it into my own ears, however, all it did was muffle the sound, and I could now hear the fluctuation of sound waves as people began to speak. I slapped the palms of my hands against the sides of my face and screamed, before knocking my chair and shrinking to my feet. Rocking back and forth on my heels, I repeated to myself like a mantra, "It's not your fault. It's not your fault." But the voices inside my head are telling me otherwise.

These voices inside my head then forced me to leave the room, and leave the room I did in a flurry. It was as if the very ground underneath my feet was convulsing, and I needed to escape before it swallowed me whole. I ran through the gaping doors, across the open courtyard, and into the overgrowth of shrubbery and trees that seemed to overtake the back portion of the school. It was there that I sobbed for the loss and futility of it all. I did not feel his loss, but instead I felt anger and a boiling envy for what he had that I didn't. Even in his death he left me with such a severe jealousy, because all I could think of was how selfish he was to take the easy way out, how I wished that I could muster up a life's worth of courage to end my own, instead of wasting the days in pure agony of wishing to be something, anything, as long as it wasn't me. The people here, the living, they needed him. They didn't need me, because for as long as I could remember, I was always much more dead on the inside than alive.

And it was in this forest that I felt his presence, and in a soft whisper that did not sound like my own, I quietly said, "Why couldn't it have been me instead?"

The Salt Stack Addresses Her Creator

They called me His wife. The one who
would follow Him anywhere. My loyalty
strong as the final pillar that fell.

Now they gather to praise the martyr.
Watch how she no longer dances.
Watch how she no longer speaks.
What honor in this, to commune with men
while I atrophy in an ill-fated tomb.

I have heard the stories they tell of my city.
All fucking and fire. All wet tongues and
damnation. So many of them are true

but I loved this place. This tinder pile.
This collection of cracked urns
filled in with gold. Zoara, the only land spared,
would taunt us, call our lives abominations
because Sodom was never meant to be understood
by gold coins or white devils cloaked
in the costumes of saviors.

When they told us to leave –
leave or burn eternally with the rest –
I fled not for me, but for my family.
The final remnants of chosen people.

I know I cannot decide for them
where their faith lies. Who to call out to

in the dark. Whether this will be an Almighty
that would gladly throw sulfur on a dream
or a demon that would dangle it
in front of them like sage on a thread.

This is what Sodom taught me.
This lawless respect. This safety
without God's hand to hold
the gates of our heaven shut.

I gathered what little I could carry
and vowed to return for nothing else,
but when we fled, I cannot pretend
I didn't carve out knots in the floorboards.
That I did not scratch my nails down the plaster
so that the dust could later be
mistaken for my body's own salt.

Everyone has heard the stories
of how I recognized who belonged
to each scream as brimstone rained down.
How I carry my heart too heavy. Now,

tell me again how it is better to stand still.
How to love a damned thing is akin
to being a damned thing. Remind me
how this punishment is divine
retribution for my affinities
and let the prayers turn sour
inside your own mouth. If I am to be
immobile for their transgressions,
stand still and say nothing for mine.
Call me by a Man's name, erase my skin,

and tell them how I am a traitor, but

do what you must to leave in peace
so I can continue to grieve a world
that not even the holy will look back to.

-C Anne Gardner

a wish list for hurtling
thru space semi alone

a blanket - because
some times it gets cold

your phone may not work out there

bring a book, something to burn in your heart on the lonely
nights

your elders and our ancestors
one dark inked permanent marker
no excuses whatsoever
bring some totem of this life you remember. an artifact

of what preceded this casual oblivion

bring an orange if you can find one
bring all this and more -

no jewelry. no extra clothing.
no bible to protect you. and no gun.

walk bravely. perhaps some one
will meet you there.

-baraka noel

Downtown Chicago

The lurid growl of tigerish hunger
In the rawboned man's eyes
Drives my mind down
To the jade impossibility
Of building homes for everyone
And packing their bellies
With work and rest and joy

The corporate headquarters
Behind me
Remind me
They rise up
Like steel mothers
Telling us to get in line
And be good kids
And sell their empty stuff
To little stomachs
Who can't even afford
The value menu

-Eric Allen Yankee

Sleep

Quiet now
Listen
Right now
It comes again
Like death
Or taxes
Another pack of cigarettes
Or Jesus
Or lovers
Promises
Of sanctions
Sex
Sleep
Silence
Laying down
And rising again

Quiet now
Before the streets awaken
While the robins sleep
When the drunks amble
Down the sidewalks
The trees start to consider
When to drop their leaves
The church lays dormant
Hobos curl up on benches in the park

In the background
The Redline and dreams
Run through it all

As prayers
Float through the sky
Trying to find their way home
Like children's letters to Santa
Justification
A place to rest
As the poet shifts nervously
The artist cleans his brush
The average man
Long since having washed his hands
Jazz clubs doors open to spill out into darkness
Somewhere

Shhh,
Quiet now
Under a seemingly Mediterranean sky
Hovering over American dirt
Lay the remains of a day
Now as gone
As forgotten
As youth
And first loves
Beautiful little confusions
Mistakes
Shh
The sound the hot breeze or cold wind makes
As it travels down Clark and Bleecker Street
Blows dust and forgetfulness over
Another flicked cigarette butt
Over baby teeth
Since healed broken bones
And first dances
The kiss

That one damn kiss
That will never be forgotten
The questioning
Of virginity
Vicissitude
Vernal realizations
Violence on pavement
Another siren driving by
That created the necessity for writing

Quiet
Quiet now
It is that moment in the morning
Where even the dark stars hide
In the citys light
The moon eclipses itself behind a cloud
So as not to disturb the otherwise silent air
The atmosphere has stopped
Accepting stars that fall
As the three killed last weekend sleep
The other thirty seven shot
Heal
There is no room for words
This is the time for
The idea of things like poetry
The necessity of it
And two bottles of wine
Being real
The reckoning
Of any of this being as salient
As much as the long since digested spices
That still habituate the walls
From last nights dinner

And finally
I close my eyes
Quiet now
Sleep
Shhh

-Gregory Curry

Pythons

Men so fat with cash
Their small eyes are slits
      Stomachs rippling
Like smooth bodies of
Androgynous
Over indulged Pythons
      Slithering along the city's edge
Splashing their saliva on
Foreclosure signs and
Rubbing their injustice scales
      To ignite firecrackers that
      Gleefully illuminate ghettoes
Built up by these Reptilian masters of
The contemporary art
      Of violence

-Eric Allen Yankee

The Heart Beats Patterns Irregular

I am
undisciplined. I
still don't listen. I
miss deadlines
and weddings, times
I should have been
sitting with my people,
whoever would have me,
all of us weeping at
two souls' union.
When you (the one)
hold you (the other)
and your dad
holds a camera.
Occasions like that.
But I'm sorry.
I couldn't go.
I got held up or lost or laid low
and I heard you did great
and I know that it's true, and
now all these babies are appearing
and I'm sorry.
I don't know what to do.
I am
undisciplined, yet my
bones glisten,
slick with the blood
that got stirred up in
a petri dish, two parts
rye, one part why not,
one hopefully romantic

night in Ontario,
Christmas nineteen seventy,
about five years out
of your air force, or
maybe my math's bad.
I always had courses to
make up like lies about
homework and goals and
applications, whereabouts
and remainders. That
blood of yours gets
pumped from my heart,
sent every second to
all of my parts, failing
of late on different
scales and timetables.
Tendons divide.
Fat multiplies,
blocking arteries. The
heart beats patterns irregular.
Leaky intestines that stretch
from my guts to the moon
if you pull hard enough
have been stopped up
and bursting and put
back together. My
steadily baring teeth.
Hardening liver. I'm
hardly believing this meat
that I'm made of has made
it this far. No job. No car. An
upright pontificating carcass
on

a
stool
at the bar. A chaos-clogged
day-dark shark tooth apartment
under two over-achievers.
Godless. I am that arsonist
of my own cardboard castle,
who's taken a match and a gas
can to every last plan I've
ever been handed. Every
extension I've ever been granted.
No Explanation.
Lacks discipline.
Has trouble focusing on the
task at hand. Can't ask for
help when does not
understand. Ties his
shoes funny. Seems to
know his colours well
enough. Probably fucked,
but good luck

                                        -O'Helloron

Are you Now; Have you Ever?

My question was quiet, but clear:

"So what do you think today about those years in Birmingham? You know, when the Klan and the Citizens' Council opposed integration?"

"Well, I'd have to say the Klan was right. I don't mean right in burning houses or churches, but people had the right to shop where they wanted and to go to school where they wanted. It wasn't the federal government's business."

I wasn't interviewing a former Birmingham police official, or a former Klansman. I wasn't in someone's office or downtown club. I was in my parents' home, my wife and baby daughter ten feet away playing tea party while my mother and father and this man's wife socialized before supper. Christmas Eve supper.

These were family friends—longtime. Their daughter and I had been friends before kindergarten, since the womb even, as old photographs of our mothers sitting on our front porch, pregnant together, attest. Through the years there were many such suppers; trips to Alabama football games on fall Saturdays back in the Sixties. Back when the crowds and the teams were all-white.

Their daughter and I went to public school together. We experienced the convulsions of integration; the fights, and the supposed harmony of our senior year when the Homecoming Queen was white, and the School beauty contest winner was Black.

Times change both more and less than you think they do.

Our senior prom was held privately at the Birmingham FOP lodge. A segregated dance at a policeman's hall. For our first two high school reunions, though, the parties were held publicly. Were integrated.

But ever since, due supposedly to the two sides disagreeing over venues, there have been separate but equal reunions, except that it's hard to say what is equal.

Much harder now than in the Fifties when anyone could see the rundown Black school and the slightly less rundown or perhaps wildly prosperous white school.

For no one on either side actually got to see the other's reunion site. The actual locale, unknown to anyone not invited. Of course, not even all white people received invitations to "our" reunion. Only a few: the proud; the elite.

Our venue was a private home, a very fine mansion in the hills south of Birmingham. Maybe it isn't a mansion, but it will always be three times larger than anywhere I'll live. Amongst the reunion selection committee was the daughter of our family friends.

"Remember when she threw sand in your eyes," my mother asks recently.

"We were only three, Mom! I've tried to put that behind me. I think I've forgiven her."

Forgiving, forgetting. But nothing is ever quite over.

#

I was working on an essay about my father's rabbi, Milton Grafman, of Birmingham's Temple Emanu-El. Rabbi Grafman was a good man. He encouraged interfaith dialogue. In a troubled time, he chose not to be an ardent Zionist. He was no racist either, yet he did not believe that Dr. King, or any outsider, should journey into Birmingham and stir things up, only to leave it all behind for others to clean up. Others, like himself and the Alabama clerics who wrote a declaration advocating that changes in Birmingham be left to

Birminghamians to orchestrate and administer. Their public letter provoked a response from Dr. King.

The one he wrote from a Birmingham jail cell. That's famous history.

I don't know how many private stories of those days still exist, published or not. But our family friend had one.

A prominent Birmingham lawyer, he was involved in the negotiations between Birmingham city officials and the Kennedy White House. I don't know exactly what he did or said back then, but he told me that times were tense, that the Kennedy delegates dispatched to Birmingham didn't understand the local problems.

I wondered aloud if anyone did.

"That's a fair point," he said. "But we had to live here."

I think it's interesting when people say things like "We had to live here." Interesting because in those days—the Sixties and Seventies—many people left. Sometimes they moved out of specific neighborhoods and into other ones nearby. Other times, they moved into neighboring counties. Suburban counties. Sometimes they moved across school district lines or into rural, county outposts.

What does "living here," mean? Exactly where is "here?"

For instance, our lawyer friend's family moved from the older neighborhood we lived in to a newer one in the western part of town. Where a newer high school was being constructed —one zoned for whiter clientele.

I got zoned to that school, too, as did Black kids from my side of town. By the time his daughter and I graduated, the ratio of Black to white students was 60-40. Over the next decade, it got worse, if by "worse" we mean more segregated. If we mean that others who "had to live here" found that they didn't.

"It was just a difficult time," he said. "Raising children back then...yes, I believed the Klan was right in that there should be neighborhood schools, freedom of choice."

"Did the Klan want freedom of choice?"

"Well, yes, meaning that we ought to be able to pick the schools we wanted our children to attend. I think you'd find back then that not only did white people want to go to school with other whites, but so did Blacks. When you force people to change, to mix, then you're asking for trouble."

#

The neighborhood my parents lived in at the time of this Christmas gathering had been changing for the previous ten years. Black families had moved into the next block. And just before Christmas, a Black family moved in next door to my parents.

And so it was just after supper, after it seemed that all discussions of race and the past had been left in the wake of our Cornish game hen meal, that my mother turned to the lawyer's wife—her oldest friend—and said:

"Well, 'they' moved in last weekend."

Her friend made no verbal response. She didn't have to. Her face contorted into the visage of a mongrel pug. And then she shivered like you do when someone scratches her nails on an old elementary school blackboard.

#

My parents remained in their home—the place where my mother grew up; the house she and my Dad were married in. Married not by Rabbi Grafman, but by a Montgomery rabbi, Rabbi Blachschleger, who sent them an anniversary card for the next fourteen years, until he died. Unlike Grafman, Rabbi Blachschleger believed in mixed marriages. It took a drive-by shooting in front of their house on a hot summer Sunday afternoon to get them to move. Ironically, they had become friends with the family next door.

Do times change? When change is imperceptible, is it still change?

So many of these figures are dead now. Rabbi Grafman, my Dad, Dr. King, my mother's oldest friend. But just last weekend, my mother called her friend's husband, the lawyer. He's in an assisted living home now. He has severe back problems and who knows what else.

"He was glad to hear from me," my mother said. "I had to get his number from his daughter after she told me he wished I'd call him some time. The funny thing is, he's always had my number. Why didn't he call me?"

Of course, I had no idea.

"He always was strange," my mother said then.

I agreed with her. We can hide from the past, and sometimes we can even bury it. At some point, though, we give ourselves away in a chance remark, or a silent action. Or in a ringing voice that speaks of "freedom," even if most of us will never agree about what that word meant back then, when things seemed so black and white. Or especially now, when they so clearly aren't.

-Terry Barr

Letting the Bad Grass Grow

To make up for deforestation, as a tribute to the wild I let the weeds grow. I only stop when the other squares of sidewalk fear the jungle.

But then I can't resist a dance of dominance over the dandelions, pigweed, buffalo burs, crab grass, oxalis, and any other animals that have entered my domain. They growl and nip at my socks.

I sneeze and dance till my ankles itch, till green juice stains the pavement, till my nose is red, inflamed, and starts to bleed.

-Ori Fienberg

Lightning

My lover is a painter, a bolt of lightning frozen in mid-air. She
doesn't want to inhabit my world the way I share hers. She
believes that words are evil, tied to paternalism, violence and
death.
She's in her studio now, working on a huge, hyper-realist
painting of people lost in a lightning storm. I'm in my study
flinging words on the page like Pollack having a fit.
Suddenly she's in the doorway. She asks: If one pukes blood,
what does that mean?

-Mitchell Grabois

Steak Knife

My little brother must have been about four
and had gotten ahold of a steak knife
while in the Schaeffer's front yard. He was
impressed with himself for causing so much
shock and concern among his friends and siblings.
He was holding the knife by the blade, pointy
end aimed pretty close to his heart. I was
eight and saw about a million tragedies play
out in my mind so without hesitation I ripped
the knife from his fat, sweaty hand. The
surprised look of pain on his face was exceeded
only by his sense of betrayal. "I'm sorry," I said,
"but this is what big brothers do." His hand and
sad eyes bled into my shirt as we walked away
and didn't stop until long after we got home.

-Richard King Perkins II

Intolerable Objects/Tomato

The first was sliced thick, watery and viscous
with seedy mire, menses on Irish thighs.

Imagine an immaculate kitchen window:
a picture show with a poodle skirt of cumulus.

Lettuce, now gored into an irreparable mess, lies
complicit on a plate, smelling of clammy nightshades.

Once I was a hothouse gone to seed
in a trailer park in Blythe, the sky

vermillion in airlessness, in suffocating
sunsets of dust and pesticides,

our food dead and gone. The dinner table
was the color of a beetle trapped in sap.

If I sit long enough, merciful troops
of aphids arrive, steady in the night, and I am allowed

to heave the scarlet filth from dishware
to toilet drain, pooling blood in the basin.

In the yard, a woman paid to care
feeds our soiled underwear to potbelly pigs.

-July Westhale

On The Dance Floor

the first time i dance with a girl,
her backside is a boom-box
i grip tightly,

bumping in perfect sync
with the house party bass line
against my pelvis.

lil wayne slurs beat it like a cop
my hands do to her back
what police did to rodney king.

i grip her shoulder like a child
finding daddy's gun for the first time
and bend her over.

i've never felt so powerful.
i mold her into a chew toy.
my dance moves be hyena teeth
sitting in the jaws of my pack
of friends behind me.

i turn around
making sure i could hear them
howling with approval.

i want to be what my peers
call social. secure what my father
calls manhood. i don't care
if she is uncomfortable.

the first time i dance with a guy,
his grin is the arch wanted
in my spine.

my joints stop
understanding movement
the way a man's desire
can ignore the word No.

his hands – a dog's stream of piss
shooting into my back
marking its territory

there are no questions
before i become his
chew toy

just heavy bass,
liquor, beads of sweat,
hyena-toothed palms
gnawing at my waist line

just let me break you off, pa.
he tells me this be all for fun.
my mouth is a white flag
wanting to shout stop.
a smile bleeds
to the surface instead.

-Joshua Merchant

The Truth about Psychosis

While underwater I somehow still could breathe
through the muffled wall psychosis constructs during sleepless
nights, the candy elixir of mania on my tongue
the rushed air of the train that's coming,
how I can't help but be its station,
and my observer standing on the last piece of dry land inside of
me restricted to its perch while waves cover my territory.
Jasmine, watch Jasmine
shed her clothes in parts in public,
draw on her walls in broken script,
send messages that don't make sense to people that don't make
sense, give away her belongings as though she has enough to
give,
speak in rage only,
not sleep for days without drugs,
kiss the wrong lips
trust the wrong folks,
starve her failed frame,
divorce her hygiene practices,
walk barefoot on broken glass.
Jasmine, watch Jasmine be a drug the architecture of
destruction, tsunami her humanity
for her village.
This is not treading water;
I am submerged in watching others watch me,
brace myself for the moments my support network will never
forget,
slow motion watch the drop of their jaws
the face of how impossible they see me in this moment,
the freeze frame I will forever now see in their eyes when they

look at me.
To touch so intimately the line drawn in condition by those
that love me most to see the sea and everything it screams
the present and the past making out in front of me,
teasing me with their sounds
their memories
their stamp.
How the ocean can hold it all.
How no human can.
How I feel like my own ocean
rip tide pulling me away from myself
toes now drenched on my dry perch.
I am activity of expectation and surprise all at once. Stigma just
like stereotypes are birthed from something in these moments I
am that something,
I am gone to them now and just water.
My old Reverend told me once that all of my poems should
come full circle that I should never leave my listeners in hell
–advice that almost stopped this poem from being born.
The truth is hell has been perfectly within my reach some days.
Truth is when things are drenched they take a while to dry out,
they are prone to mold and fungus.
I am sometimes still damp.
I will always bear the evidence of saltwater on my skin
and maintenance means buoyancy only on good days.
Hell and heaven have to make friends inside of me if I'm ever
to travel on land again.
There is a prayer in my gut somewhere hoping my listeners
still can spell heaven with my words still can see beach days in
my smile.
May that be so because they know I'm an ocean as below, so
above,

because they are proud of the way I've dried off. May that be so
because nothing is in vain
not even the climax of my movie
not even my visceral memory of shame not even my ugly
my nightmare.
For in the end I breathed through all of it somehow. For in the
end I am still breathing.

-Jasmine Schlafke

Kyle Lee

The smooth blue sky sparkled as calm, puffy clouds drifted by. The lively green fields seemed to roll on forever into the background. The late afternoon sun dragged shadows across the scene, stretching the dark spots away from me. I was wearing a zebra striped shirt that day, and I stood in front of a grassy field, past a lively creek. I run my fingers across the grass, shadows, and my younger self, feeling the cracks along the ancient photograph. I stare closer at my former self, attempting to extract a higher quality image from the grainy film. I put the crumpled photograph back into my pocket. As a child, I had never seen the fireworks. In the small community where I grew up, there were never any large events. Our family was focused on all wörk and no play, and it had made me a dull boy. My parents had never taken me to see the colorful eruptions of light burst through the dark night sky. I was never part of the cheering crowds.

The sounds of chaos waft through the air, drifting from the distant civilization to the luscious green fields where I sat, with a pair of sunglasses and a watch. Horns, sirens, wails and screams. The emergency announcement broke out about half an hour ago. I imagine the roads, tracks, skies, oceans. So many possible escape routes that mock us with the possibility of life, the dynamic of survival. But now they are are unusable, as expected during a crisis. Talk about water, water everywhere, but not a drop to drink, huh?

I slide the aviator shades over my eyes and settle comfortably into the lawn chair. Ignoring the panic floating around me, I scan the horizon, following the once green fields of crops. The slim stream next to me ripples indifferently as it quickly races downhill. I glance at the watch hanging on my wrist. 4:54 PM. Maybe forty minutes until our predicted demise, I hope.

Earth is directly in the path of Mars. The two planets had fallen into each other's paths. Some say, that millions of years ago, Earth and its little sister Mars had collided before, causing the formation of the moon. Soon, we would meet again, and similarly, nobody would be able to witness the fiery impact. A reawakening of the past, a reawakening of life in our lonely solar system.

I'm tired of worrying, I'm tired of the way we live. I'm not scared of dying. If nobody else is going to survive this, then why should I sit here in anguish, awaiting my doom.

I only have less than an hour before my doom, I'm not going to cry. I'm going to go out and enjoy something, I'm going to go and do something I have never done before. I'm going to see the fireworks.

I glance at my watch yet again, checking the time. It's now 5:21. The end draws near, as each second passes.

I see the sky, in its bright blue glow. Yet, it slowly wipes away, like the life on Earth soon will. The diameter of the sky slowly fills with the large red shape of Mars.

Eventually, the sky transformed from light blue to the reddish rust colored surface of Mars. It grew closer and closer. The atmospheric heat became unbearable. The temperature rose and rose, and soon enough, bits and pieces of debris began to fall from the heavens.

I take out the faded picture of me again. The picture's eyes glare at mine. I reflect the look.

"Have you ever seen the fireworks?" I ask.

The photo continues to stare at me with its unbreaking gaze. I take its answer for a no.

"Have you come to see the show?" I question.

The picture remains silent.

I'm not getting off of this planet. Nobody is. I might as well enjoy the show.

I lie stretched out on the lawn chair, facing west. A low purr fills the air, a crescendo that steadily drowns out the chaos coming from somewhere over the rainbow. The debris begins to fall more rapidly.

"There it is," I say aloud, gazing at the bright streaks lancing down from the sky, "This is going to be better than any fireworks show."

I push the sunglasses up against the bridge of my nose.

When the vibrant column stretches down and touches the earth, there's a pause. An isolated pocket of silence, nothingness. The showers continue, the heat increases and finally, the red planet gets closer, seemingly close enough to touch.

And here we go.

BLOOD LINE

in the story
my great grandmother
crashed her family's oldsmobile
on purpose
killing her husband
who was, they say, mean
as a man can get.
even his kindness
burnt.
even his body
made ash turned
the urn in her
living room a color
that refused
to go
with the wallpaper

outside the story
i watch her
sit before
her antique vanity
three mannequin
heads crowned
in modest wigs
all gray as an image
from a forgotten war.
she tries on each
paints youth
back into her face
before we go
for dinner

where she wont touch
her fork
for fear it will become
a car
in her hands

-Sam Sax

Tunnel No. 10: When the dust clears

Apple handed me the knife and I violently tore through the veiny twelve by twelve inch envelope. It contained a cassette tape, a gun and a note. We sat down and dug our fingers into the sand. We didn't have any water left and our teepee resembled the trimmed, scattered hair on a barbershop's floor. The last boat that we saw sailed along the horizon and evaporated on the edge where the water meets the sky. We tried to call out to it but our mouths were subdued by dirt and our noses caked with seaweed. I played the tape. The eerie music scratched the insides of my ears.

My nails were chewed down to the nub. Blood ran down my fingers from the ruts of my cuticles. Her burnt smile and temporarily squinted eyes frightened me even though I knew her from the days she chewed the heads off Barbies at age five. Our skin was scarred from the dead branches in the forest. Her eyes were drowned in her skull and my cracked hair lay dead on my cheeks. Our scalps were boiled but our eyes were cold. The light in them burned out with our final bowl of porridge. We discovered life of the homeless when we arrived here. We have lived on the outskirts of California near the Redwood forests for a year. Our coats were our second skin. Apple's veracity charged me. Without her I would be a flattened rat's carcass on the side of the road with no one to appreciate me besides young boys fascinated by death.

Apple said, "Let's hitch a ride down to the city."

I said, "Let's go." We carried our backpacks and hiked to the highway. The bitter, rocky beach offered no more consolation. We walked up the path onto a flat road, which led down to the highway. We held out our arms and waved to cars as they drove by. The eroding air bit my finger ridges away.

"The wind up here makes me feel alive," exclaimed Apple, but I found it suffocating. She took in a deep breath and blew out hazy smoke through her nostrils as if she was clearing out a sooty pipe. A matte black Lexus pulled over and a young man stuck his head out the window. He looked like the type of character who had blocked out the windows of his house with duct tape. He opened the door and said, "You girls need a ride?"

I leapt in the backseat and Apple followed me. "Guess that's a yes then," said the driver. He began to tell us about his trip to the Bellagio in Vegas and we pretended to listen. He asked if we were hungry and gestured to the coolers in the trunk. We ripped the food apart. Apple and I chugged down some Coronas and wolfed down a couple of meatball subs. The inside of the Lexus smelt like fresh meat sliced in pieces and when I examined the floor I found a backpack. Inside it appeared to be a sorority girl - hiking trip survival pack, which included an issue of Seventeen-magazine and oil free concealer. My eyes met Apple's. She drew a telephone wire through my mind and received my thoughts.

"Can you pull over at this gas station? We need to buy a few things," said Apple. "Thanks for the ride though." He said, "Oh come on just let me get off the highway first!" I reached for the gun from my bag and jammed it into his back. "Listen we're not fucking around. Stop the car or you're dead." He abruptly pressed down on the brakes. Apple snatched the shiny pistol from me and shot a bullet at close range through his skull. I threw his body out of the window and we took off in the Lexus.

"Wow that was a powerful sandwich," I said. Apple's unrelenting smile broke out into a sharp laughter. The wheels of the car flattened the road and the blue walls around us collapsed. Apple sailed on a murderous high and I absorbed her energy. The light reappeared in her eyes. Her dusty lungs cleared. Her body weight increased by ten pounds and a healthy woman replaced the skeleton that was driving before. Her hair regained its luster. My skin became smooth and my hair grew back. The fire in my chest ignited itself. We sped down highway 101.

"We should go to Vegas," she said. The red rings around her pupils spun with intensity. "Let's stop first and clean this car out." She agreed and we stopped at a discreet viewpoint. We emptied the trunk, hid the coolers on the side of the cliff and wiped down the whole interior. "We're only thirty miles outside Los Angeles, let's stay there tonight," Apple said. I turned to double check the trunk and I saw a handle at the front of it. I pulled it up. Benjamin Franklin stared blankly up at me three million times. "What are you doing back there Storm?" Apple asked.

"Nothing. I just wanted to look at the trunk another time before we leave." I replied. "Let's go," she said. We picked up some speed and then traffic hit. The rows of cars were lined up like bums who waited every month for their social security check. Apple turned on the radio. "Sometimes I wonder if the world's so small, that we can never get away from the sprawl" seeped out the speaker's voids. But we were leaving the sprawl. The crystal clear voice and innovative melody of Arcade Fire pushed the traffic through the bottleneck. We were on the way to a new identity, a new version of ourselves. We filled up the tank with gas and switched places in the car before the dreaming, drooling cashier could wake up from his wet dream.

-Cora Thornton Silver

All The Men Went

All the men went
to the mines and
my grandfather carried
a canary in a small cage.
When the bird expired he
chose to stay as the others
rushed to air.
At his funeral Mass in
the church he never
entered, a choir sang
Danny Boy that was his
drinking song. No one
understood his choice
to lay beside his pick
and sleep; but I had
spent a night in his home
when I was small and called
down for his company.
He lay beside me
and explained how
the light that reflects
through a prism is a true
division of a miracle and
this was joyous to him to
know and he described
the tracks of carts carrying coal
and the flashing lamps of fellow
gods and he recounted, touching
my hair, the Iliad and Apollo of the sky
on a knee, firing arrows in single
beams.

He was without vice: but when the
elevator ascended from the shaft
in daylight savings time, grandmother told me he disappeared to
land for sale and tasted the rich black
soil of Illinois with a spoon. I think,
and write, of ultra violet and infra red
light that vibrates in every kind of
molecule, even cloud drops, in
a music for grandfather and choice
mythology.

-Charles Bane Jr

Thrive

And his feet were weary,
Blood emblazoned on the city streets
Who could have ever known that after so much destruction,
There was still beauty on the horizon, just one more step away?

-Connor Maltby

A New Kind of Folk Hero

you're living a Hemingway lifestyle
on a Kerouac budget
cognac from a paper cup
first class jet setting charged to a stolen Mastercard
leaving war zones in every third world hotel room for
shell-shocked maids to clean up
taking every detail down on a rusty typewriter

you're willing your body into Hollywood shape
on a Charlie Sheen diet
crushed can abdominal muscles hard as mescaline
veins angled like torn aluminum
smoking cigars like shotgun barrels
catching bullets like baseballs
white powder chalk lines on a bathroom stall sidewalk
you are the American Dream's nocturnal emission

you're thinking Platonic thoughts
with a Hefner brain
lowbrow showdowns with philosophies found in flophouses
Diogenes hygiene with Aurelius attitude
trying to fight or fuck your way out of the proverbial cave
improvising the long game
breaking rules like kneecaps

you kneel before stained porcelain Madonnas
praying for a legend left unfinished

-Troy Cunio

Tempest
Originally titled "Breaking Blood Vessel"

From our compotation in the mist
Of a violent wind storm of intoxication,
I knew I would find myself moist, held
Up against a fence by
your amorous disposition.

And I greeted you with an unspoken dialect
Only you could understand. In one night, with
One breath, hungry eyes
met hungry hands.

Your tongue became acquainted by breaking the
Walls of my crevice, unleashing 100 foot waves
Within me. The fluidity of passion took hold of a
Sinking blood vessel plunging into the depths of
My vitality.

We morphed into archaic creatures. I, a blood-
Sucking parasite of Hirudinea, repeatedly latching
Onto your skin as if your blood were my medicine,
I sucked you dry,
yet I gave you oxygen--

To breathe, to live, for pleasure, for my satisfaction
Of you penetrating in between my thighs. Fingers
Pulling hair, I can still feel those fiery eyes, gazing
At my trembling body,
deciding on what limb to feast on.

I knew then, you, a grey wolf with teeth of Canis Lupus

Was on top of me. A blood-thirsty interaction with a
Throbbing heart beat pulsating through me, into me,
Ejaculating a bitter viscid solution that left an unsavory,
Unwarranted,
after taste for weeks.

-Thea Matthews